WHAT? AGAIN?

Also by Frank Kuppner from Carcanet

Everything is Strange
Second Best Moments in Chinese History

Frank Kuppner

WHAT? AGAIN?

Selected Poems

CARCANET

First published in Great Britain in 2000 by
Carcanet Press Limited
4th Floor, Conavon Court
12–16 Blackfriars Street
Manchester M3 5BQ

A CIP catalogue record for this book
is available from the British Library

ISBN 1 85754 499 4

The publisher acknowledges financial assistance
from the Arts Council of England

Set in 10pt Ehrhardt by XL Publishing Services, Tiverton
Printed and bound in England by SRP Ltd, Exeter

anD

Contents

from *A Bad Day for the Sung Dynasty* (1984)

A Bad Day for the Sung Dynasty

1
The elderly statesman trudges wearily over the bridge;
He was expected in the palace more than twenty-five minutes ago.
Surely that is not his penis he holds in his hand?
From the bedroom of a house in Germany I once saw trees exactly like
     that.

11
The volume lies untouched on the table, still open at the same page,
When, after some hours, I return to the library in the evening;
Still he sits unperturbed on the banks of the same stream;
That is probably still a waterfall in the distance.

15
Two insects descend onto the head of the great man;
They gaze wistfully across the bald expanse;
Slowly, they begin to edge towards each other;
His sudden cry of understanding frightens them away.

18
With difficulty he reaches the group of pine-trees at the summit;
Several monasteries hang on the huge mountain curtain behind him;
Noticing the exact tree behind which she pissed in the spring,
He smiles, turns to the sunset, and begins to sing.

19

Suddenly the dog stands erect in the garden;
Bamboo sprouts tall and elegant behind him;
Who is that person being hacked to pieces on an upper balcony?
This could be a bad day for the Sung Dynasty.

59

A pair of exquisite magnolias grow by the side of the road;
He plucks the one which is already in full blossom,
And tosses it through the window-screen of the woman he adores;
Four days later, the other is in full blossom.

69   *A Faded Inscription*
'Arriving very early I knocked vigorously on your door,
But an old lady from a window opposite told me
You were probably gone up the mountain to find a cool place to
        jerk off in;
Somewhat alarmed by her smile, I hurried away without waiting.'

105 *An Inscription*
'This morning, realizing I am sixty-five years old,
And have still not touched my neighbour's unmarried sister,
Except fleetingly, by accident, seventeen years ago,
I throw a furtive stone at his head as he strolls in his garden.'

120 *An Inscription*
'For five hours I climbed this mountain pillar,
Visiting your small hut in a plateaued forest,
To find a note stuck to your door saying,
You were gone for a month to a brothel in the provincial capital.'

151
He stands mournfully at the edge of the stream beside his house;
A minute ago, in a rage, he threw a manuscript into the river;
If only he had waited, or had lived further from the stream;
He trudges back to the house, trying to remember the first line.

182
With a yell of triumph he finishes the great work;
He slumps back in his seat, exhausted but happy;
Idly, he fingers through it, and reads the very first lines;
Little by little the smile disappears from his face.

231

Perspiring, the sorcerer performs in front of the Emperor;
Where has the favourite concubine disappeared to?
Trying to stay calm, he lifts up box after box,
But each of them is empty, save for a few hairs.

236

Wearily reaching his secret innermost chamber,
The Emperor turns with a smile, and notes with surprise
That twelve previous emperors are already in the room beside him;
Wearily he goes out again, to find the new conjuror.

238

How long does it take an emperor to put all those accoutrements on?
The work of a thousand hands must be about his person.
Strange that so many people should cling to him
As he wanders in solitude through his chamber of mirrors.

247

Something breasts something something bosom;
Something bust something bosom something;
Breast something something caterpillar something;
A look of doubt crosses the old scholar's face.

256

Through millions of those extremely small irises,
China was perceived, through leaves or falling heights;
Arriving on a branch amid a fluttering of feathers,
Above poets at walls, above masses fleeing in terror.

258

The judge frowns sternly behind his tapestried desk;
Another minor misdemeanour to chastise;
In the waiting-room there has gathered a crowd of millions;
He sighs, remembering when he was still alive.

277

At the far right of the room, in a recess, a canopied bed;
A single elegant foot is protruding through the curtain;
Nobody in the room pays the slightest attention to it;
After a few seconds, it vanishes again from view.

286

Seated behind a huge barrel-like hanging drum,
The court lady is cut off from the remainder of the orchestra;
She glances happily out of the window nearby;
At another window a courtier waves a sleeve.

289

A man is standing among the trees, singing,
And I have to admit I have no idea why he is doing it;
Two women are sleeping together in a nearby inn,
But that is probably a mere coincidence.

296

Now all the mountain pathways are covered by snow;
They climb sharply through the gully towards the temple;
Halted, shocked, by an approaching thunder,
They watch a tiny snowball trundle past them.

301

Every day the bridge gets a little longer,
And still the people crossing do not notice it;
The old believe it is merely advancing age;
The young believe all sorts of different things.

306

After the riotous party, they sail down the lake,
Gathering the debris still floating from the evening before:
A few hats, some torn sheets of paper,
Flowers, a major and a minor poet.

308

Since, quite by chance, she discovered that her husband
Was sexually aroused by a small rare orange flower,
She has kept the gardener busy seven days a week.
My God, what a summer this is going to be!

314

The host is weeping; the parting guest is weeping;
The servant is weeping; the boatman is weeping;
Suddenly the guest announces he will stay for a little while longer after
        all;
In the ensuing silence, he coughs, and steps into the boat.

315

Pointing to the ploughmen toiling in the fields,
The nobleman seeks to instill into his son
A reverence for the dignity of manual labour;
Having failed, they go off to view some superb anemones.

317

The last autumn leaves are descending onto the country road;
Every twenty or thirty minutes, a walking traveller;
Every hour or two, a man on a horse;
Every three centuries or so, a provincial governor.

331

A servant-girl is carrying a bowl of flowers,
As she walks along a corridor ahead of a gentleman;
In the evening, a few lights glow in the house,
And the bowl of flowers quivers beside a window.

335

The Emperor is walking along a tunnel
Which links (or so he thinks) his private apartments
With the rooms of a young woman he is rather fond of;
But, unknown to him, he has taken a wrong turning.

336

The Emperor is walking along a tunnel
Which links (or so he thinks) his private apartments
With the rooms of a young woman he is rather fond of;
His brother is following him at a discreet distance.

344

The crabs emerge quietly from the water,
Cross the beach, dig through the fence, cross a road,
Enter the little pavilion where the scholar sits,
Lift him up, and carry him towards the city.

349

In a few seconds, the tea should at last be ready;
A newly invented blend, which, for perfectest flavour,
Ought to be left infusing for seventeen years;
Frequently a widow drinks it by herself in silence.

354

There are forty-three poets here travelling in a ferry
Designed to carry six passengers safely across the river;
One cannot help wondering whether this administration
Is as sympathetic to literature as it claims to be.

356

An angry crowd is breaking into a shop,
Infuriated by the standards of contemporary literature;
The owner sits in a locked cupboard at the back,
Hurriedly jotting down a tender memoir of his youth.

360

Geese pick a low path along the wooded river,
Sometimes lower than the poets in their pavilions;
The windows are all closed in the river village;
The driving rain hammers against the shutters.

368

Half-way up the mountain stands the half-built palace,
Supervised by the half-brother of the Emperor,
Who at present lies half-asleep in his garden,
Head cradled by one of a pair of lovely twins.

384

The mynah bird once kept by the great philosopher
And cherished reverentially by his heirs
As unwitting repository for many of his verbal insights
Unaccountably goes missing two days after his death.

456

A small stream trickles through a peripheral valley,
Watched by a man leaning against a tree;
At a certain point he walks away from the tree;
The stream continues to trickle through the small valley.

476

Looking apprehensive at the centre of the procession,
She is brought to be married to the stupidest emperor in all Chinese
      history;
Yet already that evening, from the way he falls out of the bed,
She foresees that their life together will be perfectly tolerable.

477

For forty-seven years he has disdained the company of men;
He walks to the entrance of his cave and looks down to the village;
No, no, they would only look at his ears and laugh;
Slowly he walks back into the depths of his cave.

478

In a rage he tears up the holy manuscript,
Which sought to prove, at great length, that everything is illusion;
Scraps of precious wisdom flutter down the mountainside,
Creating the illusion of a flight of snowy egrets.

490

With increasing bonhomie as the afternoon progresses,
They slump beneath the willow, exchanging sexual exploits;
The smaller man describes a strange example of pubic hair which he
      once saw;
The older man lurches unsteadily to his feet, shouting.

491

Totally drunk, they emit the same giggle;
Pointing, one describes delightedly the parts of the other's wife;
Delightedly, the other does the same for his companion;
On the following morning, both lie awake, thinking.

501

The ancient pagoda has finally been deserted.
All the young have drifted away from the small island,
Leaving it only with its euphonious name;
I wish I could remember what its name was.

from *The Intelligent Observation of Naked Women*
(1987)

The Intelligent Observation of Naked Women

i
Unable to sleep, I have turned the bedside lamp on.
Did she too once catch sight of that photograph above her?
The picture of stars above my bed was surely there three years ago;
She must have lain beneath that picture of the stars.

ii
As they were before the creation of the earth,
Apparently the furthest galaxies yet photographed;
It is clear to me she must have seen that picture then;
Did she not react to the picture pinned beside it?

iii
An exquisite-faced beauty culled from a chance old magazine;
Hungarian, I think; 1965; showing a tiny breast in profile.
At one point she reared up, which was impressive, but puzzled me;
I realised later she was imitating that other woman.

iv
Surely because her own breasts were so much bigger,
I did not understand that till months had passed;
On the day when someone pouted towards a man on the continent,
How many dark-haired, unbreasted girls were walking down our streets?

v

But that night she was for a long while motionless,
Lying back against a pillow, in quiet, grown display;
Of course my eyes never lifted to the stars,
Not to the stars, not to pictures of stars.

vi

And a few sighs from a tossed head, in the absence of words,
Filled through the universe I was present in
Beyond the whispers of the nuclear stars
Breaking through their long inaudibility.

vii

A sort of starlight in a little room that night –
A small bed, salmon pink walls, heaps of books everywhere –
And particles drifting in from neighbourly galaxies,
Through the walls, through those lying on the bed, onwards –

viii

Uninfluenced, unimpressed, not stopping for the least look,
Out through my red curtains and into the universe,
Through blackness, through other rooms, through blackness,
Through blackness, through blackness, through other planets,

ix

Other rooms containing a near identical joy,
Or the last representatives of some taller race;
Ah, these interludes in the prevailing emptiness!
Such brief interruptions in the blackness, like us.

x

Not remembering the leading-up events,
But that suddenly she lay in such a giving attitude,
Her face lit by an unaccustomed confidence,
Nor how it ended, two or three minutes later.

xi

And when, enchanted by so many details,
I reached out to touch a part of her body –
A swelling cleft formed between her thighs at the sheet –
The universe trembled, and tried to end, but did not.

xii

A tentative voice from beneath the stars said, 'Please don't';
I brought back my insane, exploring hand,
Back into its own small world, landing dizzily on a sheet,
Amazed that such vast distances could be covered so easily.

xiii

The explosion at the centre of our galaxy,
Which (some say) has for long ripped relentlessly outwards,
Hesitated in its progress for a few moments,
Letting a slight shock ripple by in the opposite direction.

xiv

I think the room right next to me at that time was still empty;
I do not know who, if anyone, was in the room directly above us;
Why do I feel that, in a southern suburb of the town,
Your mother was lying awake during those moments?

xv

My past self wandered blithely through the room next to us,
Narrowly avoiding bumping into loud furniture;
It tore a picture of stars from a magazine;
It gasped, put it upon the wall, then largely forgot about it.

xvi

A sort of happy terror in gazing at such a sight,
Of course entirely unlike the joy of looking at you,
Who are not a star, more complex than a star,
But somehow this joy reminds me of that terror.

xvii

For how long did the interiors of stars
Labour to produce their earliest complexities?
A quick glance into my eyes, and then away;
There were no quick glances during that long cooling.

xviii

The structure of the female cannot but be an object of wonder;
As might befit the daughters of the stars,
Expertly inheriting the family enchantment,
Losing the sheer size, but little of the brightness.

21

xix

Or that exquisite entrance through which any daughter of hers
Would emerge into this world of light and textbooks,
Where most stars are still hurrying away from her,
And infinite nearer ones still come towards.

xx

But a lifetime's acceleration will not bring them into sight,
Even if such possible daughters do reach a lifetime;
I will not talk of them as being imprisoned within her;
Are thoughts of me imprisoned inside her head?

xxi

Behind her fringe, behind her delightful brow;
If every spark caused by me from nerve to nerve
Were to be turned loose into that other space as stars,
Would the sky above our house that night have been any brighter?

xxii

Would anyone at that silent hour of the morning,
Crossing the high bridge nearby, beside the church,
Have been amazed by a sudden luminance in the sky,
And rush home trembling, to listen to music I love?

xxiii

Or anyone caught on that stairway not far away,
Whose picturesqueness she remarked on once, months afterwards,
Have been disturbed by a sudden overwhelming blackness,
And forget for a moment his or her own ecstasy?

xxiv

Oh, hydrogen, hydrogen, why do you so assail me?
To produce helium is no doubt within your sphere,
But why produce transparent nail varnish too?
Why were the stars a preparation for this?

xxv

That lightness should become such tactile flesh;
That a whirl of plasma should smile at me;
That the throwing out of metals by a dying star
Should sit down on my chair in the morning, to put on her tights.

22

xxvi

The stars beyond pulsing their various hues,
And her wine-coloured bra resting on heaps of my papers;
That which has cradled her breasts scenting the flickers of my imagination;
Far away from this, they grow too fully.

xxvii

The intelligent observation of naked women
Is, besides, to glimpse an alternative universe;
The outline of her breasts is confirmation enough
That distances are not the only distances.

xxviii

Within touching distance is also infinity;
Her clothes discarded like our neighbour galaxies;
The ease with which she and the morning reassemble them;
The ability to open a closed door.

xxix

She left behind her cigarettes and a lighter;
I found them and, against instructions, ran after her;
I met her at the bus-stop, and we talked,
Moving back into the doorway of a shop.

xxx

The sky was blue, and feigned an absence of stars;
The pictures did not whimper inside my locked room;
My fingers weaved figures in the cool air,
Beside her body, but now only beside.

xxxi

The captain of the spacecraft passing nearby
Scrutinized the scene casually in his viewfinder,
Decided there was no sign of intelligent life,
Re-examined his charts, and went on for better places.

xxxii

Inside my room the air particles danced for joy;
The sheets ecstatically re-arranged themselves;
I bought a newspaper and took it back to my room;
Sitting on the chair where she had sat, I began to read it.

xxxiii

And the same eyes which had so caressed her body,
An arms length to the right, long hours ago,
Now ran over reports from the other world,
Seeing wars refracted by the shape of her navel.

xxxiv

I thought myself stationary in my little room;
Herself travelling back to a nearby room;
The planet moving, and its motion moving;
All things moving much as they always have.

xxxv

Sitting on a chair, reading a newspaper;
The low, soft chair on which she had sat earlier;
Which had been in that room since first I rented it;
My happiness the aftermath of who knows what feelings.

xxxvi

What grey divorces have lapped against the walls of this room?
What seas have slowly rotted into intelligence?
Where were her various sighs already by my reading?
Reverberations still rippled from wall to wall.

xxxvii

Oh, in the background to the sound of stars,
There still exists a faint remnant of noise
From the first explosion which may have started all this;
Which some believe was not the first explosion.

xxxviii

After all, I twice heard her sharply intaking breath;
So why should the universe not also breathe twice?
Space so large and dark and her arm-bangle so precisely placed;
How do we ever overcome the distances involved?

xxxix

Nearness is nearness only up to a point;
Although better by far she should be in the same room
Than lost unspoken to elsewhere in this city,
It is still a private cosmos whose foot I touched.

xl

It is still a sort of star lying beneath stars;
A star put into human, breathing shape;
A star which could choose who should enjoy its light;
A star that could think and laugh and be hurtful.

xli

A star which could disappear for over a year,
Then pass by suddenly in a street significant to us,
Throwing a normal visit to the theatre
Into a few hours of shaken recovery.

xlii

I am using her to overpraise the stars;
For no star ever had such liquid eyes;
And words developed from their careless fusion,
Some of which I wish could be unspoken.

xliii

That night we talked below a picture of stars;
A little turning planet took us into the morning;
On less than a dot to the nearest other such planet,
I whispered endearments approximately into her ear.

xliv

In whatever direction I turn there is such richness:
In the numbers of planets caught in the curves of stars;
In the number of rooms in this not very long street;
The number of hairs in the scented galaxy I drifted into.

xlv

How nonchalantly the wind rearranges her hair;
As nonchalantly as it turns into flame
Different visitors from beyond the earth;
Is there no light where her hair was strewn across my pillow?

xlvi

Or was it her whom I saw in that building yesterday,
Or one of the phantoms I mistake for her;
Her face much changed, about the mouth particularly,
But the architecture of that face remaining.

xlvii

If, on that morning, I thought of the future at all,
It was as the present continued, something miraculous;
What sort of inappropriate world is this
Where so much misery follows such a night?

xlviii

Is it three years, nearly, which have altered that face?
Something of the tiredness of her morning features
Might thus have been imitated by misfortune;
How much I would have preferred her morning features.

xlix

So much space around us, and yet we lie to each other;
So much silence, and yet we add silence onto it;
On so many mornings when I could have watched her face,
I have woken up to the pictures on the wall.

l

And I have ignored the pictures on the wall too;
I have passed days beside pictures of the galaxies
Without too great a thought of the worlds involved,
As once I spent a night, a few nights, too few nights.

from *An Old Guide-Book to Prague*

1

It being my almost invariable habit
To visit a second-hand bookshop on a Saturday afternoon,
And wander among those rearranged heaps of the past,
Rearranging them myself each Saturday afternoon.

2

And surely I can afford this little book:
This little book of photographs of a city:
Almost any city, provided I can afford it:
I shall go and ask the man what price he sets on it.

3

Three days later, I read the back cover,
And discover that the book was published in June 1937;
Before that, it had hovered among the forties and fifties;
Suddenly all those people breathe on the other side of a war.

4

The River Vltava is still approaching Prague;
At tables on terraces hundreds overlook it;
An approaching war is not so easily photographed;
People are moving to and fro from the tables.

5

For a long while I was puzzled by the precision of his stance,
On the top of three wooden steps leading up to a boathouse,
Until, decades later, I noticed he was carrying a deckchair;
Even so, surely his head still points in the wrong direction.

6

Whether that train along by the river is motionless,
Or arrived as the photographer opened his lens,
Is scarcely knowable; the road alongside is empty;
On the terrace people either move or are motionless.

7
The old man slumped asleep nearby at the library table,
With *One Hundred Years of Scottish Football* cradled against his lifting
    chest,
Was doubtless awake as quite that train drew through quite that landscape;
But, wisely, I do not intend to waken him up to ask him.

8
They are all returning from a boating trip;
Three women exist variously on the landing quay;
The eldest blocks out the bottom half of a fat bending figure;
I suspect this is a man somehow related to all three of them.

9
The flash of light on her wrist no doubt indicates a minute;
Is that the day's newspaper she is routinely carrying?
The wake of an unseen boat has disturbed the centre of the river;
Two figures at a distant table stare aghast at the photographer.

10
If the crowds were suddenly to vanish from all those tables,
Except for those who, seven years within that day,
Would have been taken away to be murdered somewhere,
A crowd would still remain, looking at the river.

11
Odd, during darkness to look at sunlight;
To look at a world without so much known history;
It is merely to indicate a busy intersection at a bridge
That these (I think) seventeen people and three and a half motor cars are
    presented.

12
Surely the absence of the Second World War
Ought to be more apparent in the quality of the light;
All I see are old cars, and coats somewhat the wrong length;
I am unable to decide even what season it is.

13
Three and a half cars inevitably provoke questions
Where a hundred would be too many to think about;
One moves in a different direction from the others;
I stare in as best I can through the light reflected from its windows.

24
I re-open the book on the next day, at last a sunlit day;
Again I observe exactly the same past sunlight;
The same brief movements still caught among the same architecture;
But what they did next is a little further away.

28
Gulls hang in the nearby air or chase the thrown bread
From a crowd of women leaning over the embankment,
Among whom two, as they stretch their hands out towards them,
Premonitorily imitate the fascist salute.

29
Outside an enchanting church named after a repentant harlot,
Huge angels gesture on top of two high pillars;
A woman passing in the street nearby is carrying a large bag;
In another street another woman carries shopping.

30
Snow lies at the foot of the statue of the hero;
A profusion of ruts and footsteps, although no-one is there now;
In the distance, on clean ice, skaters cover a large field;
On his pillar, the hero gazes far far over their heads.

31
A weak winter sun burns a bright glow on the ice;
There is just enough light to indicate the black skaters;
How many whistling falls will soon be maliciously discussed
Over dispersed meals already being prepared?

34
Strange that a shot from such high towers should be so uninteresting;
I suppose it was taken very early some morning or other;
Some distance away, past the left spire, two cars are parked by a door in a
        wall;
A further distance off, a third car is moving away.

35

I suppose it was taken very early some morning or other;
Far below, two tiny figures walk across a vast empty square,
Narrowly escaping the huge, obliterating right tower;
Probably the rest of their day has gone unphotographed.

36

Some distance away, two cars are parked by a door in a wall;
The shadow of a neighbouring house neatly encloses them;
Both contain cigarette-ends left there by the same woman;
In her own car she is now driving through an orange light.

38

So, on that morning or afternoon it was just after five to four, was it?
The emptiness and sunlit angles suggest the more probable morning,
Leaving only common sense to favour the afternoon.
I assume, of course, it is keeping accurate time.

40

Such slight marks on a wide square far away
Seem too occasional to contain a whole life each;
A woman following a man following a man;
No, the one in the middle is actually a woman.

42

This afternoon, the wide road contains about ten people;
An hour ago, three were listening to the same wireless programme;
Tonight, one shall waken, gasping for breath,
As the two little sisters lie, whispering to each other.

44

As I listen to a recording now twenty years old,
Although it was bought by me only two days ago,
I stare at a picture in a book bought nine days ago,
Showing two windows opened, thirty years before that clarinet.

46

A little swarm of people has gathered in the square,
As if uncertain in which direction to move next;
The moment's sun cools them in a black rectangle;
A shower of back windows is open in the town beyond.

47

Such tiny skylights in the roof of the castle;
So inconspicuous only the tenth look notices them;
They seem to have been burrowed out from the inside;
I see a patch of sun beside so many sleeping faces.

48

A man in uniform is walking alone up an oblique sidestreet;
He seems to look at the window beside him, grown from the street below;
At the foot of this, in sunlight, beyond walkers and two parked cars,
A lady lugging a heavy bag has just emerged into tiny view.

49

Though forty-five years later I can see them both
There is no possibility of their seeing each other;
They may have been intense lovers a year or two before;
It's more likely they will never meet throughout their lives.

50

Or they may pass each other at intervals of years,
In queues, in passport offices, in trams,
And never for one moment notice each other,
Or ever feel a long gap widening.

51

Perhaps twenty seconds earlier
The man would be more central in the left foreground,
And she, moving a few steps away in her real life,
Would not influence the chemicals in a small box nearby.

52

Perhaps twenty seconds afterwards,
She has by then arrived at that second doorway,
And the eye glances at a stark blank old street
Which someone is one step away from running into.

55

There is so much sunlight in this little book,
As if ten suns were shining on that city;
I can barely remember rainfall in my dreams;
And everywhere three or four or five windows open.

56

A surprisingly narrow road outside a palace;
A flag fluttering serenely from the roof;
That car is very badly parked, on that corner;
I think the Prime Minister was killed in that building,

61

Somehow surprising that ordinary real lives should go on
In what seem such extravagantly picturesque surroundings,
Like living on a set for *Fidelio;*
A fraudulent antique pram stands in the middle of the pavement.

62

A man turns a corner under an awning,
His left hand thrust meaningfully in his pocket;
A huge baroque church swells over the trim façade opposite;
Halfway up it, various stone men point.

67

The two visible clocks both agree in the time they show;
The crowd in the milling street has just entered another afternoon;
Watches tick on on such a procession of wrists;
Inside the houses above, various words are spoken.

70

A tree of some description coyly leans over the wall;
Two strained Titans hold up the pediment of a doorway;
From the fine door opposite, nobody exits;
An orange trundles about on the balcony.

75

A car whose registration number ends five eight dash one six four
Is parked near a building with a fascinating overhanging window;
The window is open and piano music drifts out of it;
Many of the crowd walking below look up as they pass.

76

How callous architecture is – such little nostalgia for horses;
Each day for thousands hoof–clops reverberated off every one of those
        houses;
Now, above the screaming and the smell of automobiles,
Their curtains signal to each other as impassively as ever.

79

It seems from the captions there is a notable building in this picture:
The problem is, I am uncertain which it is;
That bare wall above an arch? That drab façade at the dustcart?
Surely the photographer is facing in the wrong direction?

80

The dog trots confidently down a narrow crowded street;
A girl exchanges light and darkness in the arched arcades;
The man in uniform limps by a statue on Charles's Bridge;
In twenty-five minutes they ought to be together.

85

A long straight busy street reaches for minutes into the page;
More life within it than in a thousand books;
Even to count the dots is an insuperable task;
As soon manage to enumerate the windows exactly.

87

There are four tramcars, possibly five, in that long deep street;
Four or five drivers, four or five destinations, eight or ten coaches;
Only one of the trams is actually approaching me;
It is unlikely to be entirely empty or entirely full.

88

How many, scattered throughout the branches of the city,
Now stand at precise points, simmering in anger,
Having recently just missed one of those four or five trams;
They scan various distances for oncoming traffic.

89

I suppose someone there is driving a car for the last time;
How much nonchalance are those small vehicles carriers of?
Or the wild joy of driving your own car for the first time,
Lost among those impassive rows of traffic.

90

That dot there will kill some people within five years;
That dot runs his eyes over a newspaper;
That dot seems to huddle wearily against a huge building;
That dot halts by a car, letting a tram pass.

91

A high white suburban building stands on a remote hill;
A two-horse cart is impeding the car immediately behind it;
The driver sees one tram and neatly spaced cars approach, and cannot
overtake;
He looks up at the white building and sighs, if he can see it, which I very
much doubt.

92

This dot here is troubled by two of his teeth;
This dot is passionately in love with that one there;
That one there is about to buy a favourite cheese;
This dot here is the merest speck in the distance.

93

Car after car is parked by the side of the road;
And it is not even, I believe, any particular day;
Many kitchens and bedrooms are having their constituents altered;
Knives are being sharpened, life insurance policies bought.

94

Thirty seconds afterwards, that tram has disappeared;
That man is no longer in the shelter of an awning;
So many lives are in slightly altered positions;
Women move in rooms on the sheltered side of the street.

97

A precise wreath of white smoke drifts out from one of the chimneys;
Far behind it again stands the centuries-old cathedral.
Now that she has managed to get the fire started successfully,
She goes into the next room to read the latest letter from her mother.

98

What scents drift outwards from the row of little shops:
Coffee, cigars, bread, leather, violins,
Enterprise, consistency, contiguity, morning;
A plume of white smoke eddies down towards them.

99

If the happiness in those stone houses were plumes of white smoke,
And the unhappiness therein similar plumes of black,
And on this fine summer's morning all the windows were opened,
The philosophers would hurry to Zeltnergasse.

101

The white dot in that archway is surely only a blot on the paper;
If a bulb, I cannot see what it is suspended from;
And why shine a lit bulb there in the daytime?
A woman walks along the tramlines underneath it.

102

A woman leads some children before the steps of the Parliament;
Two of the littler ones have gone on slightly ahead;
At this moment, in the neighbouring country, Hitler begins to play with
    his penis;
The little boy is to the left of the little girl.

103

It is five past four in the afternoon again;
The church here would be perfectly symmetrical
If another clock were where that slim window is;
Urgent bronze soldiers are alone in the wide square.

107

The sense of Sunday and a listless, fleeting crowd;
The familiarity of this distant scene haunting me;
Some of my German relatives must be here or hereabouts;
Oh, silver nitrate, silver nitrate, how much I have loved thee.

109

Not exactly that wall, not exactly those lines of light,
But something very similar, decades afterwards,
Looking out of her back window, on to a church,
With the same sense of being too close to its walls.

111

Three little girls are passing under an archway:
What is it like to be a woman of fifty?
In the house which one of them is running towards,
He sits on a bed, holding a pair of her socks.

113

A tunnel has been drilled through the base of a legendary hill:
A man and woman with a pram are about to enter the tunnel;
An adult and a child have almost reached the light of the other side;
A sunlit distant house calls through the absent mountain.

116

That terrible ease with which the unrepeatable occurs;
A number 8 tram swings past the number 11;
Two gentlemen in the middle of the road converse solemnly;
A van parked at the side of the road has its door open.

120

He sits on a bronze horse, resplendent, holding a lance;
Below him, a tramcar curves around the monument;
For some reason, I am reminded of the view from the steps of St Paul's;
In fact, at that moment, walking down the steps of St Paul's –

121

The gardens of the Agricultural Institute
Are overrun by mothers with prams or children;
There is also a huge heap of sand in the foreground;
On the heap the shadow of a mother walks with her child.

122

The new technical school is still impressively modern;
A clock shows a quarter past one near a hole in the façade;
Two women push prams through vast empty grounds;
The windows behind them suggest an occupied dining-hall.

123

While three large naked bronze men grapple beside a bridge,
A man upon a motorbike pulls by beneath them;
In the white car beyond, some fairly harsh words are spoken;
A hundred typewriters clatter in the Electricity Building behind.

124

As the two women walk across the bridge side by side
The wind blows their coatflaps into identical billows;
Each has her right foot extended in front of herself;
My father is nearer to them than my mother is.

125

The Faculty of Law seems utterly deserted;
Its stern archways seem thoroughly unscrawled upon;
A single blur passes in front of its chaste wall,
Just well enough defined to suggest female clothing.

126

A man is standing outside the Ministry of Defence
As inconspicuous as the Venus de Milo;
At the moment probably no-one is being tortured there;
Two schoolgirls are almost out of the picture.

127

Window after window on the spare clean modern building;
Is Czech being spoken behind every window?
Behind how many windows has Malay been spoken?
That one or that one or that one?

129

I sit in a library, looking at a photograph of a library;
I inspect the caught positions of the passers-by;
How resolutely they cross streets forty-five or forty-six years ago;
I hear the traffic on the road outside.

130

There is something in the precision of that motor-cyclist,
In the middle of a wide road empty of traffic,
Which almost makes me feel interested in such a form of transport;
For a fifth of a second I feel that perhaps I have missed something.

132

The trolley-bus is running past the expensive houses;
An old lady is fighting her way up the long clean street:
On one of the roofs stands something very like an entrance portico;
The photographer quickly takes the picture before he sneezes.

138

From the strange low splash of sunlight on part of the theatre façade
I think we may deduce an unseen archway opposite;
If there is a road there, there are people on that road;
Some of them must surely be moving away.

140

Huge angels flutter on the roof of the theatre;
Directly below one of them, at ground level,
A woman smaller than their wings is reading a poster;
Tactfully, the angels are gazing elsewhere.

141

He has stopped, alone and motionless in the park;
He stares intently at a newspaper;
Thirty seconds of his life are washed away in that surprise;
Then he hurries towards a modest meal of vegetables.

145

I feel that sort of building would surely have been familiar to Schubert:
It looks sufficiently old, and similar to his birthplace;
Not so familiar perhaps would be the black stain on the sky;
No doubt he often lay looking at stains upon the ceiling above him.

[145a

And retyping these lines for a book some sixteen or so years on,
It occurs to me that the month I spent in Vienna before I was twenty
Is still the nearest I have ever been to these old streets;
Those which are still sights, and the sites of those which have gone.]

148

Perhaps merely brushing the dust off his jacket,
But he seems to stand on a very busy pavement
In a curiously declamatory posture;
Two clocks above him agree it is half past one.

149

As she strides hurriedly across the busy road,
Her light taut dress clearly indicates the shapes of her legs;
Good God, so all these women possess legs, do they?
This puts an entirely new light on the situation.

150

What fine invisible lines must stretch out towards each other:
On one floor of the building, a café;
On a higher floor of the building, a café;
The clinking of so many coffee-cups.

152

A tram trundles by outside the café;
He leans his head over in her direction;
On the floor above is a language-teaching institute;
Those trees have the bare look of late autumn.

163

The wooden gate in the dappled sunlight has been opened;
The thin high stairway stretches out behind it;
Its upper reaches vanish amid overhanging trees;
Only a broken twig falls from step to step.

164

Two men are walking towards the archaic wooden church,
But one gets the impression they are not going to go inside it;
One does not get the impression where it is that they are going to;
But one gets the impression they are not going into that church.

168

On the far side of the bridge, the neatness of a formal château;
On the near side an unkempt wilderness;
At no point does there seem to be a gate;
Doubtless there is a gate, but we do not see it.

169

I shudder to think what revels were carried on
In that odd, brutal castle, abruptly rising through foliage;
I suspect, though, that they did not involve Thai girls;
All the Thai girls who were dancing were dancing elsewhere.

170

The castle has taken leave of the village below,
Higher above the trees than the clouds are above itself;
As easy to walk to the moon as to that uppermost row of windows;
A few unread books lie in the various rooms.

171

With the whole street indicated in electric lines,
A tremulous old lady is standing at a corner;
At least, I get the impression she is tremulous;
Possibly she is of a thoroughly resolute disposition.

172
Every twilight, the city has departed;
It has crept away into the tourists' memories,
And its quieter sister has slipped into its place;
The next day it returns, with a slight hangover.

173
Lights are on the statues, lights are on the porticoes,
Lights are on the monuments, lights are in the towers;
Lights show at most of the windows in the streets;
But it is the lights in the windows that go out first.

from *Movements in the Crypt*

5

As he hurries through a vault of dark columns
Towards the lights at the far end of the cathedral,
He hears an occasional breathing behind some pillars.
So: still they have not got rid of all the temple prostitutes!

He hurries behind a pillar. Nothing is there.
But the breathing seems to be louder now. He hurries
Behind another pillar. Nothing but breathing.
A light hand reaches out towards the back of his neck.

9

A rather large virus is creeping over the mountains.
Four distant men are splashing about in the water.
Someone well-dressed is sitting on an island,
Writing a book about rather common illnesses.

Oh, do not say Loch Lomond was never exactly like this:
It is all a question of detail. Four Scandinavians
Watch people balancing on rocks, who think they will be alive tomorrow;
A doctor laughs as he writes a letter in a speedboat.

15

A muscular body sprawls forward in heavy slumber.
A genteel hand holds the head by its long hair,
Taking care to avoid the blood spurting from its neck.
Light draws its valleys on her own attractive neck.

Far below the picture, she is still asleep.
Why did she choose this image for her bedroom wall,
I ask myself as I crane towards it, forgetting
That I have slightly mistaken the identity

Of both the woman in the bed, and the image
In shadows above her. Yet, I gaze down at that
Delicate nose, delicate eyebrow, other
Delicate eyebrow – all so vulnerably

Visible – and all so familiar to me,
And to several of my close friends. Again I must fight
That atavistic urge to tamper with
My expensive thermal underwear (the season

Being once again the onset of winter) –
But, with a scream, I vanquish these temptations.
A professional burglar cannot afford such weaknesses.
Quickly but carefully, I throw into a plastic bag

Her breaths, perfumes, odours and deodorants,
Communications from redheads, photographs, attempts
At describing in prose how unforgettable were
A forgotten morning's half-dreams, followed by

Something so obvious that I need not name it here,
Then a green belt and a few favourite memories
Of her childhood, and a few favourite names
Intended for her non-existent children.

Clutching a foot as a souvenir, I then take
One last judicious look round the room, listening
To the almost intensified breathing, and, thinking,
'How different it could have been,' slam the door shut.

18
Bones of previous failures lie littered at his feet.
The threatened town lies beyond him in the valley.
Oedipus, playing desperately for time as he thinks,
Is inexpertly tickling the breasts of the Sphinx.

He has, so far, discounting ambiguities,
Given seventeen wrong answers to her riddle.
As he hesitates before delivering the eighteenth,
She says with a sigh, 'Your fourth answer was correct.'

19

A distant lighthouse flares out over a nearby sea.
A knight on top of a type of bird is spearing a dragon.
A naked young lady is chained by the wrists to a wall of rock.
She turns herself tastefully as far as possible towards him.

The picture-frame is also tasteful. And, just below it,
A failed public transport official shudders joyfully
On the stomach of his sister-in-law, who cries out
'I am lonely!' enthusiastically in her native tongue.

Meanwhile, the abstracted spiritual essences
Of the previous owners of the house, stroll about,
Pocketing whatever valuables they can find.
What an amazing thing is the human mind!

20

This picture once hung on my mother's walls, I think –
In a different house from that where she lives now.
That same strip of sunlight in the middle distance;
That spire repeatedly interrupting the horizon.

Today, for what reason, I finally lose patience with it.
I deposit it among communal dustbins, where
It half obscures a torn newspaper, whose headline
Talks of a crippled man murdered at sea.

23

A few books lie at the back of the complicated library.
Some men groping towards them are fading into the air.
The attendant sitting at the table looks at them and laughs.
He returns to reading a slim volume about time.

I enter, fifteen minutes late as usual.
We exchange a few words of insincere banter –
Just enough to incommode the readers nearby.
I deliver my final plagiarism, become

Instantly serious, and cross to where the books are.
I shake them open one after the other.
Money drops out of a few, and, of course,
The occasional long-since-invalid ticket

For journeys back to distant invalid parents.
Gathering together the books I have chosen,
I build a large room out of them, close the door,
Throw myself onto the bed, and pretend to snore.

27

The woman in that portrait reminds me of my grandmother.
The hazy world which memory places her in
Seeps back unhampered to the century
Where old women shout at the youthful Vermeer.

I do not remember her ever shouting at me,
Though my sister has different stories to tell. Only
On that solitary occasion, when I climbed
Onto a chair, from there onto the mantlepiece,

And thence up onto the highly elaborate mouldings
Which ran round the four walls just below the ceiling;
And hid snugly between two petrified ferns
For almost an entire day, which caused her to panic,

And encouraged her to haunt the local police station,
Where she was strikingly insulted by a large dog
With personality problems, had her money
Purloined by a confidence trickster dressed as Liszt,

And lost most of her hair, before she escaped.
When she discovered that I had, all this time,
Been ensconced among the decorations, capable
Of witty, elusive conversation, she at once

Removed a thick belt from her waist, and furiously
Flicked out at me with it. This must have continued
For an hour or so, until with a resolute gesture,
She tore off her skirt and pursued me even more eagerly.

I ran for safety into the Art Gallery.
That is where I always went on such occasions.
The large skeletons, and models of extinct animals,
Are such solid productions, that they provide

Ample space to hide behind for as many
Of the neighbourhood's children to do so as might want to.
In the evenings, we would emerge from our hiding-places,
And walk up to the adults who were waiting for us.

34
That nymph is reclining in such a buttock-flexing position,
It is difficult to believe she is really asleep.
Sumptuous fabrics are ruffled on the ground beneath her.
I sit on a cushion in the garden, leafing through a book

Of Chekhov short stories in charming but inadequate
Translations – smiling at what I believe
To be endless tiny distortions of what it was
The man was trying to say. Is she asleep?

I look over, but cannot make up my mind.
In a neighbouring garden, a few loud children blame
Each other for the unsuccessful end of a game.
Oh, the snow is flowing on the steppes; the young women

Are getting teeth extracted unnecessarily;
The bishop is contracting typhus. I look up.
The nymph has got to her feet and is walking towards me.
She is a little fat, by contemporary standards,

But then, so am I. And I lack even
The courage to expose my dignified torso
To the sun, lest I alarm the neighbours. She,
On the other hand, brightens up the whole garden

By her brilliant skin and lack of inhibitions.
Indeed, the light reflected could be called dazzling
With little exaggeration. She says a few words
In a French dialect, and then translates at once.

'My name is Virtue, and you are looking at me
In a most peculiar manner. I must go now
To wash some potatoes in a sink up there,
Behind that window.' Saying which, she pointed

With her arm to a window not far above me, and with
The attendant breast to a room at present occupied
By an ex-officer in the apocalyptically
Rearranged Polish army; whose exact rank

Has been told to me more than once, and, more than once,
I have quite forgotten. At that exact moment,
He was lying on his bed, thinking of snow
Falling on wounded crows near Suwalki, with

Tears in his eyes, and a digital alarm-clock in his hands.
I was glancing, with foreboding, at the nearby lane.
'I see you are looking at the lane,' she said.
'I need hardly remind you of the symbolism.

However, if anyone should come in from the lane,
Looking for me, you must on no account
Tell them either that I was here, or where
I have gone to. Do you understand that, Jim?'

'What sort of person?' 'Any sort of person.
Korean, or wearing armour, or with the typical
Dull eyes of a misogynist. Do you understand?'
I nodded my lying agreement, and she departed.

A coolness at once established itself in the air;
And the children playing in the garden opposite
Began to be noisy again. A few hours passed,
But no-one came in from the lane. At several moments,

Bored by my reading – no, not exactly 'bored':
'Alerted' is perhaps more accurate – I went out
Into the lane, to see if anyone was there.
On four or five occasions, there was no-one there.

But, once, a man was leaning against a wall
In a manner so obviously preparatory
That I hurried back inside, sprinting to reach
My grassy cushion before he appeared. And sat down,

Imminently expecting his arrival.
An hour passed, full of non-appearance, and when
I peeped into the lane again, I found
A familiar emptiness. An emptiness

Devoid of possibilities. This disabused me
Of all remaining expectation of success.
Returning, I detoured to the very spot
Where I had seen her earlier that afternoon,

And picked up the abandoned fabrics, still there,
Spread luxuriously out, in what was now
(For the sun, as usual, had moved) the combined shade
Of wall-top and branches. I gathered them in my arms,

Causing a major commotion among the discarded
Twigs and leaves; and the bare lawn all at once
Became exultantly empty. I carried the bundle
Through a combination of cool passageways

And open doorways, until I reached my room.
Once there, I stripped the clothing from my bed
And replaced it with the coverings I had stolen.
I then glanced at my watch, washed and smartened

Myself up, and strolled into the town.
That is to say, a fifteen minutes' walk
Over a bridge and past a few mansions,
To a pleasant public house, constructed in

Various styles, standing on various levels,
Where women, not necessarily carrying knives,
Appear at the end of the day, having crossed
And recrossed their frequently exquisite legs

In offices usually slightly to the east
Of where they now sit, sipping alcoholic
Beverages, and laughing as they watch
Other people's reflections in the mirrors.

35
The taste of liquid is famously hard to draw:
Only that joy of the first or second gulp
Capturable for a few seconds, in the most living works,
With sudden plans to visit the local greengrocer's.

And when one gets there, they are of course shut;
Obeying some local law, axiomatic
To foreigners, but a mystery to you.
Homesickness reflects from every newly-cleaned window.

40
How can one be sympathetic towards a century
So full of younger sisters locked in the attic,
Whose tentative yelps for help are mistaken by passers-by
For birdsongs? We all know birds are different.

They eat worms, and do not wear necklaces;
Nor, hearing a heavy step on the stair outside,
Do they gasp with fear, look round furiously,
And run over to rattle the locked windows.

49
In the abandoned dormitory, the soldier
Rises and turns. He does not yet realize –
Perhaps he never will – that this time
No-one is coming back. Illness

Influences the mind strangely. As would
The image of the beloved, lying neatly on her bed,
Stretching out her leg, straining to touch
The nearby telephone, which is at present silent.

from *Five Quartets*

I

i

The light, such a distance away from its source,
Had finally to negotiate a window-blind,
Where, but for that accident of a month before,
It would have found no gap for such a bold entrance.

ii

And, having so resolutely forced an entrance,
It would have drawn that same long line across the room,
Even if at no point on its trajectory
Had it picked out the hand which it did pick out.

iii

And so we have, one morning, light picking out a hand,
Unobserved by the possessor of that hand,
But looked at by a person on the outside of her dreams.
Her dreaming head is beyond the line of the light.

iv

I placed one of my hands beside hers,
Not touching, not like the evening previous;
As close as possible to hers, but without disturbing her;
Then moved it away, looking at the distance between them.

v

The light, such a distance away from its source,
Deflected from its emptiness
To draw a line across a carpeted floor,
Across the extreme edge of a table

vi

On which there lay a still open copy
Of a record booklet for, of all things, *Fidelio,*
Bought earlier that month in a busy shop,
Closed during those moments, with so much silent music.

vii

Her closed eyes face her illuminated hand,
But she does not yet lift it towards her face
To set the seal on another instance of laughter:
Not yet, but within six hours perhaps – .

viii

Her dreaming head is beyond the line of the light,
With its knowledge of languages unknown to me,
With its shapes from infancy in another country,
With its memories of three hours ago,

ix

When that hand or the unseen hand
Unexpectedly touched my ear, when the spinning earth
Was otherwise addressed, and this arriving morning
Invented crowds in the city where she was born,

x

Where there were streets which her conscious mouth might describe.
But she lies, cut across by a line of light,
Almost motionless, while, far within her,
The survivors of absurdly passionate multitudes

xi

Continue on their hectic route to failure,
While she seems motionless, thrashing their ways
Into a body utterly distinct from mine,
And yet beside me, touched at the edges by light,

xii

As I lie waiting for light to abandon her hand,
Or for her to move her hand out of the light,
In this morning which, precariously established elsewhere,
Shines light on a planet of torturers.

II

i

I asked her what she had been dreaming,
But she did not take the question seriously at first.
Even when I warned her that her silence
Might be seriously perverting local literature

ii

She merely smiled and wiped her cheek with her hand.
Soon she decided, 'I never remember my dreams',
Moving around in a long blouse made in Thailand,
And slippers which no doubt lacked a similar provenance.

iii

Ever since, towards the end of my monotonous schooldays,
I was handed a magazine by a French teacher, now dead,
Who may have lived in the religious house nearby,
With its cool privileged afternoon corridors,

iv

Which contained some photographs of Thai women
In Western clothes, yet of legendary elegance,
I for fifteen years considered Thais the type of all beauty,
Until a single TV programme last year

v

Described, in lacerating detail, what was happening
To Vietnamese refugees at that moment on the high seas –
At that moment or the next, she turned and told me
She could now remember something from her dreams.

vi

Moving within a fabric made in Thailand,
Directly stitched, perhaps, by exquisite hands,
Or from machines controlled and ordered by exquisite hands,
While her own hands, scarcely less delicate,

vii

Take a couple of eggs from a box,
And crack them open. Their sudden interiors
Pour and drip out, into an existence
Not as two slightly comical unflying birds

viii

But, within minutes, to become foodstuff
On ordinary plates, while she attempted
To remember more and more details of a dream
In which an uncle was talking to a dead aunt.

III

i

At last, the well-polished television set
Displays, as has been promised to us for weeks,
Some pictures of an imagined nuclear war,
Harrowingly portrayed by harrowing actors.

ii

I sit, watching fictional horrors,
And turn when she enters the room
Seeking out something needed for the kitchen.
She exclaims, 'Is that still on?' and leaves.

iii

Soon, I get up and switch the set off.
I return to my seat, and sit quietly
In a room now grown preternaturally peaceful.
The pictures on the wall reassume their former existences.

iv

From the kitchen every so often there drifted in
The sound of one plate clicking against another,
The sound of a few footsteps suddenly resolute,
The sound of a cough, and a few more footsteps.

v

I sat, hoping she would re-enter,
Perhaps intrigued by the novel silence,
While I tried to reflect on the images lately seen,
Terribly aware that I ought to be terrified.

vi

Again there drifted in from the kitchen
An interrupted succession of trivial sounds;
Distinct enough and significant enough
To suggest a new planet is being built.

vii

When, later, I look across to where she sits,
One foot lightly rapping against her half-discarded shoe,
I understand that, as we quietly sit there –
One of us appearing to read a book,

viii

The other of us really reading a book –
The calm air around us is still full
Of the waves of nuclear catastrophe, and beyond
There lies a space, punctuated

ix

By irregular wandering projectiles, large enough
To dismantle the earth at once, which, doubtless,
We would hear about if it grew imminent,
But which seems far enough away at the moment,

x

As I sit there, surreptitiously watching her face,
Framed by her hair, framed by a supporting arm,
In a room where two mouths breathe and two clocks tick,
With an infinitesimal time-difference between them.

V

i

I am somehow present in this earlier world
Of rocks and liquid; a large quiet star
Returns to turbulent waters day after day after day,
Or to light ripples, playing to no apparent purpose;

ii

And I assume, from inadequate, long-forgotten reading,
That each of the chemical constituents of my body,
From whatever warps in the brain encourage me to say this,
To the slight transient mark below my left thumb,

iii

Are present somewhere here; that these things probably
Neither favour nor dissuade any legitimate future;
All multiples of a thousand million years
Equally pointless to them; our largest cities

iv

Sway inside the water; and the water
For however long it remains largely liquid
Will not burst into tears, drifting time away
In a series of impressive discolorations,

v

Impressing no-one; dying with a red star
Into powder, striations and heat; to vanish
Without a word being spoken, taking with it
So many voices that never break the silence;

vi

Huge opposing armies disappear within it,
Their differences indistinguishable; dead cities,
Living cities, the hours of boredom,
The discovery of flight, all are suppressed,

vii

Or, if conditions in the atmosphere
Vary by a fragment, time passes again,
And lo, they appear, the novelists, law-makers,
Suicides, wits and jailers, and the long long succession

viii

Of moments believed to be ordinary: a door opens,
And a woman enters, breathing, looking happy, bringing
A few words rescued from the not noiseless seas,
And the alternative to a heated powder

ix

Which the cup of milk in her hand is; over us
Beat the crests of narrowly avoided oceans,
While we drift our way through waves shocked into existence
As that brick wall outside, that overgrown hedge,

X

Some passers-by, a van parked among the cars,
With men in wheelchairs patiently sitting inside it,
And then, towards evening, from the room above,
The renewed howling of an extremely bad-tempered child.

VI

i

I glance at my watch again; it seems impossible,
But surely she is at this moment surrounded
By unconvincing metals and glass, in the air;
I look at the shop window across the road,

ii

But I cannot place my reflection; I wait
For a suitable gap in the traffic, then
Dart across, not looking upwards, towards
The only shop in the neighbourhood which sells

iii
My favourite chocolate; how intense
The occasional aeroplane can be in the morning
Passing by overhead, and drowning
The radio playing tactfully at my bedside;

iv
Then climb the quiet, tree-lined hill,
Taking me a little nearer to the air,
In which she, my unique reference (I assume)
In a fuselage full of unique unknowns

v
Is at the moment talking or silent –
Breathing anyway – while I, walking,
As if I expect the sky to change its colours,
Stare upwards, biting through chocolate.

IX

i
I am seated at the table, turning one page after another,
Inspecting my newly bought, old battered book
Which explains long-dead dinosaurs to recently dead children;
And wondering which propositions are still accurate

ii
And which have long since been deduced
To be laughably inexact, in one of those
Numerous discoveries or rediscoveries
Which seem to feature every week in the newspapers,

iii
And ought to be followed, but never are, or are
And are promptly lost sight of; leafing through the pages,
Trying to imagine one of these creatures as as real
As the gigantically improbable schoolboy

iv

Shuffling along back lanes, being late, losing
Vital entrusted letters, trying to outmanoeuvre
Ominous gangs of loitering youths, which I was
When this book I hold was mint-fresh – what was I saying –

v

As I was seated by the window, turning one page after another,
She put a cup of tea down on the table beside me;
And then, seeing or imagining some misalignment,
She reached over, and, touching the cup at the rim,

vi

She made it resettle in the well of the saucer, looked
At the book for a moment, gave a beautifully non-committal
Smile, and left. Soon I began to investigate
What might be called the hands of the dinosaurs,

vii

But I found it an unrewarding exercise.
One or two had notable forearms
Clutching in the earlier air, or lifting
Squirming examples of the soon to be extinct

viii

Towards their emphatic teeth. Most, however,
Merely indented the unexcited mud
For the billion steps of extinction, covering
The earth and shallows with infinite pathways

ix

Towards forgotten goals. For how many days
That skin adhered to our own rocks, how many
Pebbles they knocked aside accidentally,
Not watching where they fell. We do the same,

x

My darling. But sometimes we also stop,
Halfway up the steep hill near the Arts School,
And look down to the main road behind us,
Where a crowd is moving past in either direction.

X (alternative)

i

The door is open; I stand at the open door,
Looking out, late at night, into the street;
It is not a major street, but, even so, it is not empty;
Across the roadway, a group of three or four people

ii

Make continued progress around a slight corner,
Moving away from me, talking among themselves;
On the near side of the street, opposite them,
A woman is also walking away; this

iii

Is the woman I probably love; and therefore
Some moments of chemical extravagance
Within my motionless head commit me
To watch her until she disappears completely.

iv

In a few seconds she has completely disappeared,
Loved or not loved; and an immaculate silence,
Having seen off this most recent brief challenge,
Returns a moment before its return is noticed,

v

And practises the end of the universe,
Quite without rancour, merely to pass the time,
Among the demoralized, unsleeping cars;
I expect I shall re-emerge, in a few hours,

vi

Beneath an apparent absence of stars, into
An only slightly confused echo
Of these few lines of cars; however,
For the moment I have no resource left to me

vii

But to accept that her footsteps in the next street
Tap a code which I cannot decipher, and return,
After a few brisk steps through two doors,
Into the room which she has left so recently;

viii

To discover, fifteen or twenty minutes later,
Scattering a slowly thickening disbelief
That she has ever been here, her umbrella
Left forgotten on the bed. I pick it up,

ix

To grip what she has gripped; which sheer forgetfulness
Prevents from now being her accompaniment,
In a further street, in her own room already;
And the clumsy movement with which I lean over

x

To lift it, disturbs a book on the bed –
A recently bought, remaindered account
Of a perfectly sane man, imprisoned
In a psychiatric hospital for years.

XI

i

Just outside the window, there arises the sound of raised voices;
How loudly they must be talking, for me to notice them;
One of her feet, shoeless, is on the chair beside her,
Unconvincingly pretending not to be music.

ii

Gradually I am learning more about the necessity of frills;
Another volley of loud syllables outside;
I trust all her footsteps have been accumulated somewhere,
As they ought to have been, and their distance into the stars.

iii

Pretty toes are of course a necessity of life,
The basis of all good design. A more distant shout.
We were right not to walk over to investigate.
It was always most likely they would go away.

XVII

i

Some sort of dream about a mosque; a doorway;
I lie in bed, struggling to remember details;
Near the theatre I visited yesterday
Such a building is being constructed. It is not yet open.

ii

And, even when it has opened, I trust
Neither of us will visit it; so, how
Did I manage to reach so high; all the more so
That I don't remember opening a single door.

iii

I turn my face towards the wall,
The still cool wall; lying on one side,
I trace awkwardly with one of my fingers
The little plaster bumps whose purpose

iv

Escapes me, but is perhaps merely decorative.
It was a bright day, and death was out of the question.
I was talking near the top of a large building,
Arabic in inspiration. I turned myself round

v

And groped a hand out onto the bedside table.
She is still a long journey away from me,
But a glove of hers has remained obediently
Within touching distance all night. Was she with me?

vi

I remember people in the streets below,
Passing like backgrounds of silent films. Of course.
She was there in a long warm baroque street
A little earlier. Where did she go to?

vii

Dreams disappear from the same memories
That lose realities. All her appearances
Inside my brain, from whatever source, seem so miraculous.
In days she disappears; at night she disappears.

viii

Shortly afterwards, I abandon these phantoms;
I get up, and walk towards the sink
To prepare this morning's tea for a man carrying
Vanishing dreams and a small ordinary glove.

XX

i

So much has been abandoned here by the previous owners;
Each step she takes on that still newish carpet
Echoes a hundred steps of theirs, whoever they were,
Those unconvincing people, who confused

ii

A time for arriving with a time for leaving,
And now appear to have left this place for ever,
For grossly inadequate reasons. It is no use
Giggling at some unseen mishap in the bathroom,

iii

For I am in a mood to be ridiculously literal-minded,
As I stand beside the window, with one hand
Picking at a coloured flaw in the paintwork,
And the other inside a pocket, manipulating

iv

An earring she was wearing last week. How old
Is this building? Less than a hundred years?
A little less, I suppose. And in this room,
Where first I gripped her with deliberate intent,

v

And with fingernails slightly too sharp, how often
Have outmoded fashions conformed to similar postures,
With equal freedom of movement? Oh yes,
It seems quiet enough now, as a bedroom

vi

Seems quiet in the early morning, and houses outside
Pretend to be nothing but stone; however,
If this room were the large, scarcely readable novel
Which has languished beside the telephone directory

vii

For over a week, for nearly a month, then we two
Would be no more than the sharply drawn but trivial
Characters who, on page 503,
Linger disconcertingly long in the public telephone booth,

viii

Talking and laughing to the unknown, while
The obscure first person narrator, detached
But with less than infinite time at his command,
Tightens his grip around the gun in his pocket.

XXII

i

Above me, a neighbouring child cries in the night;
Above it, the stars seem silent. I switch on the lamp,
And lie, looking at the intercepting ceiling,
Which does not interrupt enough. I check the time.

ii
The child cries on, not yet convinced of time.
There will be no sleep for either of us for a while,
But he at least has the warm possibility
That the door of his room will open, and a human being

iii
Will descend on him, with sympathy and nipples,
Which the room below him lacks. I lift myself
Onto my elbows and inspect the occupancy,
Its deficiencies by now glaringly obvious,

iv
Then relapse onto my bed, as the overhead
Whine hits a new peak. Why so much crying?
I will remember this exorbitant wail
Longer than it does itself. How much now

v
Do I recall of those first thousand days
Upon this flagrantly old planet, when I,
So well equipped for another life under water,
Or in the air, or in five times this temperature,

vi
Had to adapt slowly and with shrieking impatience
To this over-precise locale, where food
Was never ideal, darkness too common,
Absence too lengthy, and furniture

vii
Implacable in hard-edged hatred? Nothing.
We die and are reborn at some point,
And a child, left trustingly with us,
Disappears. And thus it is we are able

viii
To reach out wearily to a heap of tapes
On a bedside table, insert one in a machine,
And let the throats of sopranos contemporary with my grandmother
Obliterate a nearby noise by more distant ones.

XXV

i

The artificial milk swirls in her coffee-cup;
She takes two or three steps across the kitchen
To replace the tin; the surface of the liquid,
So recently in contact with her actions,

ii

Settles down into a less disturbed
Centrifugal whirl; in its vortex
A lighter quality accumulates
And intensifies into the precarious strength

iii

Which it ought to maintain for several seconds
Until the current equalises out,
And it dissipates throughout the cup – or something
Thermodynamically not dissimilar.

iv

There is nothing terribly unusual about this;
She returns to the table at once, and sits down.
However, as it happens, yesterday, at a loss
How to spend a particular dead half-hour,

v

I turned on that television set,
And caught an earnest old gentleman discussing
Astrophysical questions. The illustrations
Of dust slowly revolving into homogeneity

vi

As planets or stars, profoundly impressed me.
Such a typical product of the vastness
And sensational accident-proneness of the skies
Was not something which I expected to see

vii

The next morning, reinterpreted
As the froth on the top of her cup; nor that,
Watching her take three tentative, heat-threatened sips,
To the ruination of that precarious universe,

viii

The echo of the collision of stars would be there
In the slight moisture dragging against her lips,
And, looking at her hand holding the cup-handle,
I would be told how compact universes are.

ix

When a few minutes had passed, she took the cups
Over to the sink; she washed them through
Briefly; she nonchalantly inverted them
And left them to dry; a few drops of water

x

Fell down their outsides; a small pool formed quickly;
Somewhere beyond the window, larger pools were forming;
Within which, in time, equivalent people would caress,
And lick a different flavour off each other's lips.

XXVI

i

The dress she wore so memorably yesterday
Lies, cruelly abandoned, on a kitchen chair;
At first I failed even to recognise it,
Lifting it up to create a space to sit down in.

ii

So, today the limbs which activate it are mine,
Holding it out for a few seconds in front of me,
At roughly the height where she would be,
Proving thereby the utter inadequacy of air,

iii

Then throwing it with an unfelt casualness
Onto a large uncomfortable chair not far away,
Where it melts instantly into the appearance of mere cloth,
Ordinary fabric, a fabric like the chair;

iv

While perhaps its owner is striding through an office
Where I have never been, carrying
The dying traces of a night's kisses
Among the inexpertly manned table-tops,

v

Those wooden habitual fragments of her life
That unseen dreams must weave their way among;
Or is talking to some beset parental figure
As I casually throw the dress onto the chair;

vi

As close to her body as that chair is to mine,
Although I shall not have seen them when she opens
A door in the evening, with them still valid in her thoughts,
Made tired by strangers to me in this my city;

vii

And the day drifts to a closure of normal happiness,
A confusion of yawns, forty-part choruses,
And the removal of underwear; until morning
Repeats its beautiful but unfair performance,

viii

And I may pick up, in near repetition,
Whatever it is she is at present wearing,
Beyond my sight, under the same cloud formation,
Which others can see; and none of them, I hope,

ix

Are as horror-struck as I am by the thought
Of the unrecorded changes of her past,
Unseen clothes discarded through changing sizes,
Such beautiful lost clouds; and for a moment

x
I feel it is not a properly-ordered world
Where such objects disappear, while old bones
Fill postures, unwatched, in the nearby museum
From long before humans, and human clothing;

xi
And on most mornings she passes by outside, utilizing
A far more compact bone structure, clad
In soft flesh, love and clean knickers, going
To help someone whom I do not know.

from *Ridiculous! Absurd! Disgusting!* (1989)

from *The Opposite of Dreaming*

I

I do not think I have ever noticed before
These strange trees growing in the kitchen
In the early, somewhat absent hours of the morning.
I had felt something of that coolness before,

But never seen those shapes. They seemed to challenge me
To seek to explore their heights. And I stood there,
Gazing at their gloomy, waving branches,
Feeling that same sense of wonderment

Which once I experienced in the Brazilian jungle,
Standing among the gay small-breasted tribe
Which I had hoped to lead to safety, but who,
At the first sign of any danger, dispersed,

Leaving me on my own. No! No! I said:
This time I have learned my lesson – and walked past
To the cold water tap not far from the window.
I turned the tap on, and the shining water

Obediently flooded out with less
Silence than was consistent with that hollow time:
So near to midnight, so near to the dawn,
But not in the same world as either. I held out

A glass container to obstruct its flow;
And, possibly, gather in some of it as it fell,
An object in which I succeeded. Although,
Lifting the shining liquid to my lips,

I was struck by the strange aspect of the street outside.
The trees seemed larger, and the boulevard
Curiously silvery – and a man
Was lying beneath a bright car nearby,

As if fixing it – although no sound
Seemed to travel through an atmosphere capable
Of carrying such sounds, had they been made.
Fervently hoping he was perhaps not dead,

I turned back into the room, examining
The curiously precise pattern on the carpet,
As it shimmered slowly in the unshimmering light.
It seemed to show some sort of animal;

Or perhaps merely a plant; or perhaps
An episode in history which I
Was never intended to find out about.
At just this point, the kitchen door opened

And the human being who is closer to me
Than all other human beings, did not
Enter the room. Instead, her sister did.
That this came as a complete surprise to me

Hardly needs to be said. For, though her sister
Was someone whose existence was known to me,
Her position in another, cooler time zone
Had, until then, always seemed unalterable.

'So, you are the person I have heard so much about,'
She whispered conversationally, thereby
Dispelling the slight aura of fragility
That clung about us. 'No,' I replied softly.

VII

Not merely is the food in the refrigerator
Frozen, by and large, but also those moments
Of something so like happiness, with us
Standing disposed around the refrigerator; one of us

With her smooth hand on its smooth top; the other
Almost watching the sunrise, like the news
That we had incontrovertibly won a fortune
In some lottery or other, spread

As happiness would spread if that sensation
Were an atmospheric effect; which, of course,
Some say it is. Needless to say, we spoke.
Fugitives darted from our mouths, astonished,

Into the immaculate breeding air, stopped,
Looked round, and adopted the camouflage
Of remarks about trains, eyesight, and the extent
Of life before glaciation. I shifted my weight.

She shifted her weight. The almost inaudible mechanism
Of the machines that run the universe
Surged a little into hearing. We looked at each other,
Wondering if each of us could hear the same thing,

For the engineers are usually so careful
To keep the inner sounds suppressed. Our looks
Crossed, and missed each other in the crossing.
A hand reached into the refrigerator,

Extracted a previously opened carton of milk,
Let a little of it pour out into the air,
A bright, floating emulsion – and replaced it
Inside the fridge. When had I wakened up

And felt a light full breast brush against
An arm that I belonged to? Doubtless doubtless
Centuries ago. No large funnel opened
Above my head, and no milk poured out of it.

But the fugitive, who was sheltering in the room
In a clever hiding-place, took advantage
Of the thunderous overwhelming noise caused
By this potential tumult, to

Hurry in turn to the five cupboard doors
Disposed about the room, releasing
People whose presence there I had only dimly
Suspected. They all left in a group,

Whispering among themselves. I woke her up,
Accidentally, with a touch so reticent
It ought not to have awakened even her skin.
Almost at once, she began to use her voice.

I heard her speak, and then heard her voice walking
Through one doorway after another, until
It was coming back to me by another route.
I was not far from a window, listening

To the ordinary morning being glued
By her tremulous voice mixed with the cold air
Onto the outside of my skin, which the whole day
Would not be long enough to shake me free from.

XII

By dawn, the smoke has almost disappeared.
Entering a new hemisphere via an alcove,
I stand in the early returned light, feeling
Amputated limbs come back to full use.

A few stubbed cigarette ends lie still together
In an ashy stone dish. They brought to mind,
In their fragile and not quite perfect unison,
An inept litter of newly-born small animals.

It gave a shock additional to the shock
Of the morning's coolness, to see them lying there,
Inert, as if they had had more to do with
Volcanic extinction than with her neat mouth.

71

I noticed, at the rims of the cork tips,
A round of tiny blue stars encircling
The white paper. This seemed appropriate.
Outside, a blue sky had wiped the stars away,

But some stars, I suppose, were still behind it.
I conjured up her present embodiment,
Perhaps moving, perhaps motionless, in a
House twenty minutes' walk away. The distance

To the sky is of course a closely related subject;
And out towards the stars are travelling, oh,
It staggers me to consider how many signals,
Including those few sagacious scientists

Who were remembering Germany, in tones
Which included disbelief, while we
Were seated on those cushions not far away,
Being disrespectful towards our ancestors.

What careful words about the slaughter of millions
Beat noiselessly out to, over, through, and past
Various dots, mostly noiseless themselves,
In that poor audience, the cosmos – strange

That those who are not listening to us should surround us
In all directions. I remembered her presence,
Here so recently, with a shock, as one might remember
The depth of the universe, if one were God,

And had been playing, absorbed, for a few million years,
With his neighbour's spouse, or a few cigarette ends.
She was here yesterday, I said, staring
At one chair in particular, at one

Particular glass, almost but not quite empty;
At one mirror of overwhelming nonchalance.
Wisps of smoke started to emanate
From all these suspicious objects, whom I had not

Hitherto suspected of jealousy, or of
A waning desire to participate in the
Reality of the world. What choice do we have?
The amorousness of the biosphere,

(I thought to myself, standing in the increasingly
Murky apartment, gazing around as if
Expecting to hear her voice), seems to involve us
In notorious misjudgements and stupidities,

Caused, if not quite by the fact that we are not rocks,
Or by the baffling, undeniable attractiveness
Of certain not even especially expensive
Imported items of clothing, with imitations of

Wings on the subtle fabric – but, by this time,
I could no longer overlook the fact that the contents
Of the room were disappearing one after the other
Into small wisps of something very like smoke;

Or curiously like those hair-curl filaments
Which I have admired in books, littering space:
The remnants of an explosion, or the beginnings
Of a creation – I forget which – I had always

Half assumed they were half-accidental products
Of imperfections in the process of reproduction.
A pulsating glow was still discernible
From the fiery ends of the clouded cigarettes,

A near recapitulation of one of the few
Constellations I could confidently identify
In last night's sky; with an extra member added
Somewhat to the right. Without losing my nerve,

I groped my way towards the telephone,
Intending to call the relevant authority.
But at that moment someone was calling me,
For the phone started to ring almost before I reached it.

XVII

In the precise delirium of being alive
Under such circumstances, as improbable
As finding, tight in the palm of the hand one morning,
Only a few of the few hundred thousand years

When invisible fleeting organisms were the sole
Living part of this nothing planet, I reached out,
Seeking, purely by luck, chemical discharges,
Intelligence and memory, to locate

What someone lacking my ability with words
Would be forced, abjectly, to call 'one of her nipples'.
The effect was startling. We all know the dazzling
Insurrection of artificial light

(I trust) into a night so black and settled
As to seem impenetrable – but this was,
If anything, more implosive. Immediately
A highly unconvincing sun rose beyond

A drab line of high grey buildings, including
A dirty garage and a dirtier church – not to mention
A few dozen dark slumbering domiciles –
Orioles sang, and the few people in the street

Grew and became witty. I withdrew,
For an experiment, my ethereal fingertips,
And a darkness instantly returned. Now she woke up
And invited me to kill her if I wanted to.

This, I thought, is surely the language of love.
Surely, I thought, this is the language of love.
What else can this be but the language of love?
I left the door to the other universe half-open,

And thought, yes, this is surely that precious language,
Before sinking into the strange exhaustion
That so often accompanies our happiness.
The morning arrived, excreting cool air, as usual;

And an irrational sense of hope, as usual.
I leapt out of the bed, and embarked upon
That unrigorous sequence of exercises
Which I once devised, to enable myself

To allow the new and still inexperienced day
To absorb me into its bloodstream with as little
Disaffection as possible. Up and down I jumped,
Up and down, then again up and down,

Then again up and down, then again
Up and down, then down and up, then up
And up and up and up and up and up,
And up and up and down and up etcetera.

XX

In this stupendous city, where the most popular form
Of public transport is or are the magnificent trams
Named after famous local archaeologists,
Incorrigible as they sway round sharp corners,

Usually only two or three decks high –
But some of the newer, more finely honed models
Reach up to 19 or 20 consecutive
Strata of travellers – of course, those intending

Short journeys only would not have had time to climb
Too far up the internal ladders – and I
Was travelling from the heart of the metropolis
On a long, diverting radius to the west,

Having just returned from a triumphal tour
Of some or other foreign country. Ah, how naïve
These people are! And yet, how touching is
Their frenzied acclamation, I will admit it.

I was faring towards one of the suburban villas
Set up by my disreputable, but, I am convinced,
Ultimately innocent uncle; whose desire was,
Having seen how certain people in the Orient lived,

To recreate a little of their relaxed magical existence
Behind high hedges and, of course, soundproofed walls,
Reinforced by strategic bursts of music
From tastefully hidden loudspeakers – it is a duty

I have freely assumed: a pledge sworn to
At the old reprobate's deathbed, in the presence of
A few sombred relatives, and a disconcerting
Giggling sound from inside the shower-room.

Occasionally I glanced down to the streets,
Those polite chasms, occasionally I peered into
The lofty windows we drifted past, smiling
In a fun-loving, yet somehow mature way,

At any little indiscretions which
My gaze happened to witness; occasionally
I admired cloud formations with an expert eye –
It is a hobby I share with my young nephew,

Who hopes some day to travel much nearer to the sun.
The recent discovery of small white buttons in the sky
Excited both of us greatly. Myself more than him,
I rather suspect; for I know what love is.

But enough of this hubris, as my mother used to say
Whenever she bought a new gun. The point is this:
I was glancing casually out of the tram window –
It was a fourteen-decker, but I prefer

Not to travel so close to the top that all sight
Of the street below becomes etymological –
Or entomological – either in fact will do here –
Take my word for it – besides which, to be too near

Those lethal overhead cables evokes in me
An emotion which, in another human being,
Would probably be called 'fear'. And so it was
That I happened to glance away from the pornography

Which the young lady in the seat in front was writing.
The lower street, which, scarcely a moment before,
Had lain impassive and empty, now held a figure
Moving towards us from the next corner.

I knew at once that this was the woman I loved.
Well, no. To be quite honest – I merely suspected it strongly.
I had already seen her a hundred times before,
But never before on this utterly unimportant thoroughfare.

With what a shock I recalled that she in fact lived
Not three minutes' walk away from here. I gave
An involuntary shout – of joy, I suppose –
Causing the female on the seat in front

To assume an expression of genuine irritation.
I did not notice this look, as I was already
Past her, on the way down to the outside
World, if that is what it was, and therefore

Was spared the sobering task of reflecting
That details of my happiness might incommode
Other people. When the doors fell open,
And I was one of the throng let loose at that

Particular point of the city, I ran ahead
To that light-bead of the road where she now was walking.
It seemed as if some kind hand had removed
A normally indispensable barrier.

I ran up to her, and tapped her on the shoulder.
The interval between my so doing
And her eyes turning to look at me, was enough
For a new city the size of the present one

To be built on the ruins of its ancestor. I smiled.
She smiled too, but at something happening beyond me.
'I have been away for a little while,' I said.
'You said you would ring me. Do you not remember?'

'When was this?' she asked. I racked my brains.
'One hundred and thirty-seven thousand years ago,'
I eventually replied, in triumph. 'That
Is all in the past,' she said. 'It is over now.

I thought that was clearly understood between us.
You are not very quick at understanding things,
Are you?' she asked. 'I have destroyed your letters.
The only ones I made much effort to read

Were the illegible ones. Stop looking at me like that.'
I looked across the road, and saw a shop window
Reflecting, among its transience of cars,
The torsos of two figures, as abstractedly

As if it were a pool reflecting clouds
On an earlier or defunct planet. A small man,
Grinning wildly, appeared to be standing beside us,
Taking a close interest in the predicament.

I aimed a back kick in what should have been his direction,
But made contact with nothing. A moment later,
She struck me ferociously on the bare temple
With a small bust she was carrying, of Speusippos,

A Greek thinker of whom very little is known.
I could dimly, through the derailment of my senses,
Hear her running off into the distance,
Past the large statues of Shakespeare, Tang Yin, and myself,

Which, with a dozen others, including some astonishing
Omissions, stand grimacing on the façade
Of the nearby library – the lowest floor of which
Houses an echo chamber, where high explosives

Are comprehensively tested. As we did so,
She cried out, 'Taxi!', 'Help!', 'Sunlight!', 'Perverts!',
'I am being pursued by a human being, I suppose!'
I began to follow her, but at once recollected

The legal precariousness of my situation.
I stopped, and struck up a conversation
With a man who was standing by the side of the road,
Watching the proceedings with great interest.

Shortly after he dropped dead of old age,
I tore a button off my shirt, tore up
The ticket I was holding, smiled, or failed to smile,
And hurried homewards as quickly as possible.

XXIII

Across from where I stand at a tramstop in the
Incipient rain, are lines of curtained windows,
Behind one of which, or somehow escaping from one of which,
There gives out the typical blue-white flash which indicates

That someone has just taken a photograph
Helped by artificially added light.
I am intrigued by what seems the almost equal
Possibility of a blinding obscenity or

Visiting elderly members of the family,
Caught in a laughable posture of surprise.
However, the rain continues to batter down,
And soon it is already impossible

To believe I did any more than imagine even this
Nondescript unlikelihood. The rain continues.
How sadly the day has declined into normality,
I thought, since that odd moment this morning

When my neighbour called out exultantly
As I bent to pick up a starving eohippus
From my front doorstep – how obviously he
Had waited for his perfect opportunity –

To tell me, with, I thought, excessive self-
Complacency, that he had just won
The Nobel Prize – was it the Nobel Prize? –
For physics – was it physics? He had managed

(Or so he claimed) to do something astonishing
With the shape of time. I forget the details.
His explanation was too garbled by joy
To be clear enough to an outsider. 'Everything

Must change utterly now!', he shouted to me
As I hurried back into the house, already
Considerably behind schedule. 'Everything!
Everything! Everything! Everything!'

I did not know that this was how scientists behaved.
I wonder if he is still deliriously shouting
That rather treacherous word, at his exact
Point in the amorphous suburbs. While I

Stand at this rainy bus-stop – or, rather: tram-stop –
Or, rather: thin concrete strip, set against
An endless sea, becoming even more endless
With every moment that passes; fervently hoping

That the drunk man on the opposite side of the road,
Who has emerged, swaying, in a doorway,
Scratching himself in the area of the genitals,
And apparently uncertain in which direction to move;

Looking abstractedly towards one horizon,
Then swivelling his gaze round to another,
Now scratching himself somewhere about the chest,
And disappearing back into the building.

XXIV

When I woke up, my head was surprisingly clear,
Considering how enthusiastically,
And, I hope I may add, how untypically,
I had imbibed a wide selection of the contents

Of a nearby cool cabinet, to celebrate
Either the return of a local independence,
Or the arrival upon earth of intelligent
Extraterrestrials – it was a wild cry

On the street outside, I think, which awakened me.
In fact, it did not waken all of me.
One of my arms, lying underneath me,
Had grown numb while I snoozed. I lifted it

A modest height above the table, using the extra hand
I possessed, a hand still strangely operative,
And, watching with detached interest, let the corpse fall.
It seemed to hit the table shortly afterwards.

An odd feeling, to watch it slowly descend,
Strike the wooden surface with a loud thump,
Then rise into the air again. This sequence
It repeated several times. Most disconcerting

That there should be a tenth of one's own body
From which one is in exile – as I occasionally
Have remarked to my dear wife under other circumstances,
With a slight revision of the arithmetical

Aspect of the phrase. She is, fortunately,
An understanding woman, as she has need to be;
– For, more than once, when I have fallen asleep
With her fingers held against my face, or her toes –

It is largely a question of mood – she has woken up,
To complain – no, not complain – to let me know
The limb which separates her from those exquisite
Extremities – or, perhaps, connects – is utterly

Devoid of feeling. Under such circumstances,
One calls to mind a bright sunlit morning
On a planet not yet supporting life. What distances
Open up so casually. I am amazed,

I said to the doctor who had sprung to life
From his seat at the window, when my flying arm
Had knocked the glass from his hand, I am amazed,
I said, as he scratched his head, trying to certify

The cause of death – I am amazed that women
Ever allow us to touch their genitalia at all.
'Do they?' he replied. I dropped the subject.
He dropped my arm. The movement wakened me.

A woman's fingers were held close to my face.
The morning, scattered among the scattered furniture,
Was making not the least attempt to be plausible.
'I was dreaming I was being born,' I almost said.

That would have been a dream that all of us have
At some time or another, she would have answered,
Had the opportunity arisen. Her real words
Were far more interesting. In the distance,

A baby was screaming, in one of the neighbour's rooms;
The sound would have been inaudible to us,
Had we not been motionless. 'Listen to that.
I sometimes wonder if it will ever stop,'

I said, intending to refer to the baby.
I kissed her hand, and its grip tightened slightly.
What interesting expressions can fill all our eyes,
As we drift lost among the high numbers.

from *The Autobiography of a Non-Existent Person*

IV

My family greets me as I arrive, opening
the stiff door with practised, easy grace. What joy!
At least, I suppose it is joy. From outside,
in the street, thereabouts, sounds of
shouting children. I take out of my pocket
a few chiliads made of chocolate, and
distribute them unfairly to my adoring
offspring. Then I blithely regale them with
tales of my own youth. What laughter fills –
I almost said 'Hot laughter fills' – their eyes,
their ears, their mouths.

                'You are so like the sperm-whale,
Father,' says one of them, 'which, unlike
most inhabitants of the ocean – whom we
erroneously suppose to be inhabitants therefore
of all the ocean, instead merely of the niches
and nooks which support them – travels
round and round and round and round the world,
ignoring those brief exemptions to its basic
matière, which we call land, but it does not.
For to them the entire ocean seems sufficient,
and all the multiplicities of horse-drawn travel
which once existed, do not in the least concern them,
nor their suppression by other forms. Boom, boom,
go the big guns; but only for certain ears.
Can I have some money to buy some more chocolate?
These new cream-filled quasars taste just wonderful.'

'Be off, deplorable infant, ere deserved
irritation seizes me, perhaps the cause of
most of those bouts of parental assault which are,
it appears, so sadly common on this planet.
I refer here not, as you might think, to the male
mole-cricket of the family Gryllidae,
who will contentedly chew his way through his offspring

till the female intervenes – for, being lazy,
he sees no need to travel far for food
when such lies close to hand – and, besides which,
he has poor eyesight – nor to the polar bears,
noble beasts, but apparently with the same
culinary unconcern – their eyesight is superb.
No: merely to one of those quiet, unheard of interludes
in the lives of civil servants, heads of state,
and window-cleaners, sometimes within the shadow
of a superb church, and, more frequently, not.'

Such was the answer I had intended to give.
Instead I said nothing, having just been blown up
in an explosion in the centre of town.
The shockwaves slightly rattle one of the cups.

V

Thus: I had been pacing
the insultingly non-committal corridor for
absolute hours, marvelling at
its bizarre supposition of normality –
when a jubilant group rushed through a swinging
doorway (not the one
which I, from time to time,
had been anxiously eyeing; nor the one
which I had discovered barely a minute previously,
extending my increasingly nervous walk
as far as the turn of an ultimate, heroic corner).
'Congratulations!' they shouted – which I took
to be their way of congratulating me.
I inferred from this that the birth had been successful.
'And the child?' I enquired. 'What of the child?'
'Oh, have no worries on that score,' purred the Official
Reassurer. 'A perfect birth. Could it have been
more exemplary? No. Not even if
it had been following an accurate textbook;
which in a sense it was.' Overwhelmed
by calmness and relief, I lay down
on the sea-bed, and let a familiar current

swirl round me. For an hour or so. Afterwards,
I stole into the birth-chamber. How can I
already have forgotten how beautiful she looked?
Light reflected into the room from the windows
of the opposite house, or of the opposite houses.
Her expression was a striking mixture of
exhaustion, eternity, stupidity,
satiety, musicality, and lust.
Her charm too I should have mentioned. And infinity
also, I suppose. If, when she looked at me,
she had claimed not to know me, I could not
have found a convincing counter-argument.
I looked at the first child. It seemed beautiful.
The second, too, was enchanting. The third, I confess,
I was far less taken with. However, the fourth
was utterly adorable. I could go on –
but the wish not to be boring (the most truly
civilized wish for a man in my position)
prevents me from enthusing individually
over all 12,988 of them.
I knew my duty. I went over to some shelves,
and started to prepare their food. I was about
to nourish the first when somehow a stray mastiff
slipped in, seized the child, dragged it away,
and ate it. Struggling to master an understandable
sense of loss, still holding the tiny bowl
of tepid, approved mush, I moved at once
towards the second child. But a loose wheel
rolled through the doorway, struck a glancing blow,
and killed him outright. Such grief being indescribable,
let me merely say that, after a while, the morning
took on a certain predictability.
Not that I ever quite grew able to guess
the particular means by which any particular
possible child would be truncated of
its optimum or intended span of life.
But that such a truncation *would* occur
I never doubted – and occur it always did.
Number 7,255
for some reason escaped – and grew up
a credit to us all – a biology teacher

in a fine school; from whose office the view
of a small tight charming stairway never fails
to delight me on those rare occasions when I
am allowed to observed it. Oh; and number eleven
thousand and sixty-three claims to be happy
only 35 minutes away from here by a fast train;
but I am uncertain how genuine this happiness
is. And perhaps two or three more
also evolved. It is difficult to remember.
After all, we must ensure survival somehow.
The world is not a baby's toy.
I forget how often I have alighted at this stop.
I drank that every day for years, yet do not remember its taste.
Oh, this street leads to a long row of houses.
And this street leads to another long row of houses.
Look there! Look at the bubbles which fly up from them
into the air, or the ocean, or whatever it is
that they find both necessary to live in and
trivial enough to ignore. You say that others
must feed on them; that from their disappearance
emerge much stronger races – perhaps even
more exquisitely well-attuned species –
so that others can feed on them – so that –
so that – so that – so that – so that – so that –
but I say that I like this light, even
this sense of people drifting past unseen,
and certainly this music on the radio –

VI

Raging, I slammed the door behind me. The sound
excited some of the few stars still visible
in the stinging blue sky of morning: one of them
flared up and fell in a slow silent curve
above a neighbouring roof. This prodigy
startled a butterfly clinging to a petal
in the tight sunken garden. As I began
to climb the three steps to the roadway, where
my iced-up car was parked, I saw the insect
hang for an instant, irresolute, before

embarking on a migration which would take it
to another end of the continent. Its legs
were easily broken, its wings astonishingly fragile,
yet it engages on the greatest mass movement
of any known animal. Now the woman I love,
having already discovered my absence, runs out
through the doorway in pursuit of me. I stop her.
I pointed to the butterfly, and said:
'Can we too not learn from this intricate creature?
Look! In autumn, its eggs larvae and pupae are all
frozen by the first frost. Unless the adults
migrate to a warmer climate, there will be
no perpetuation of the species. Look! Over there!
They gather in swaying swarms to begin their fraught
trek to the south. In spring, they flew back again,
found milkweed plants, and laid their eggs on them.
They do not long for important people's daughters.
This seasonal migration of a butterfly
is one of nature's most baffling mysteries.
They do not exchange acrimonious letters
with people who pretend to be civil servants.
They can see for only two metres ahead.
And those who migrate have not lived long enough
to have migrated before. Unexplained winds
might pluck them from their course – there are so many
storms raging elsewhere, throughout the duration
of their passage. Yet, they fly unerringly
for three or so million metres to a place
which they have not yet visited.' 'Shut up,'
she replied, grimaced tearfully, and rushed back
with her loved and impeccable sense of direction
into the house. I chose to remain outside,
marvelling at the light. The supernatural
absence of other people also attracted me.
One is so rarely allowed to see this street
under such unearthly conditions. Occasionally
an item of traffic disrupted the main road
not far from where I stood. It solaced me
to reflect that I could prove to them how pointless
those journeys were, if I had wanted to.
I re-entered the house. No sign either of her

or of the children at first. What does it matter?
I am used to their little pets and sulks. I looked into
a few kitchen cupboards, and other such places,
for something to eat. Whatever came to hand
I unthinkingly consumed – too lazy to trouble
to prepare anything elaborate for myself.
Only much later did I learn from the horrified
and (to be honest) stunningly vituperative
reactions of my wife (if such she still is)
that I had in fact eaten some of the children.
I was sorry, of course, but what is done is done.
Besides which: not *all* of them had been devoured –
enough, at least, to build on. Endless tears
and recriminations were hardly likely to help,
were they? She knows my eyesight is poor. I did not
enquire who had survived, and who had not.
There is rarely much point in raking over the past.
Things could always have turned out differently.
Has she herself made no mistakes? I doubt it,
And some of those children were not wanted in the first place.
Besides: why have so many? Is it not simply
risking confusion and heartbreak? She should have given them
a room where they can play in absolute safety.
No. I refuse to shoulder all the blame.
Once is enough. I refuse to continually
be made to feel guilty. I simply turned and left.
I strode tight-lipped past the protesting figures,
and, raging, I slammed the door behind me. The sound
excited some of the few stars still visible
in the stinging blue sky of morning: one of them
flared up and fell in a slow silent curve
above a neighbouring roof. This prodigy
would have startled a butterfly which was resting
in the tiny sunken garden, had one been there.
But nothing seemed to be there, save me. I flicked
my wings behind me, flexed my legs once or twice
at the knee, and pulled myself up into the sky.

VIII

It was morning. I was standing by the window
admiring the charming combination of

passers-by and absences of passers-by
on the street far below – more accurately
a small square – even more accurately

an irregular heptagon. So many apertures
for a car to whizz out from; for a pair of horses
to disappear into; for a trio of deer-flies,
which can fly at half the speed of sound for short

distances (albeit only the male
of the genus Cephenomyia) to traverse
the entire vista, from entrance to exit, in less than
a second. I am all the more gratified

in that the morning sun reaches me here,
whoever I am; whereas my lower neighbours
are quite in the shadow of that vast official

edifice opposite. Only in late evenings
in midsummer, can any directer sunlight
cast as much as a long thin strip on the wall

behind their grinning daughters or tight-lipped sons.
A knock at the door summons me. I turn round.
They have come for me at last. How altered
the ordinary sunlight seems now. Oh, all this trouble

because of hydrocarbon derivatives in water.
That is to say, life. We stroll down the paltry stairway,

chatting in the most civilised of manners;
ignoring the various marks on our genitalia,
painfully acquired over the past few nights.
A few guards hurriedly emerge from behind pillars,

taken aback by our sudden reappearance,
and ignoring us punctiliously. We stride through

the miniature but impeccable entrance-hallway,
past statues and an empty plinth – no doubt
not yet occupied by its intended user –

over a strip of carpet which modulates
into an even richer one, of identical
length, when we reach a stairway. On little chairs

of ferocious elegance sits an occasional
social unfortunate, whom we pretend not to recognise.

Our eyes might meet, I suppose. A vast light
floods through the window on the stair-landing,
too painful for us to gaze through. We went on,

down a charming corridor which overlooked
a secret inner courtyard, in which played
frightened and contented children. Oh, with what joy
we lifted aside the red chord slung across

the panelled carpet-passage, to prevent
the intrusion of outsiders! On we went
into an exquisitely appointed room.

The doors at the opposite end seemed to bang shut
as we entered ours. We paid that little attention.

An air of lavender and/or opulence
came off the elaborate, well-upholstered chairs.

We lolled upon them, or tried to see our faces
in the scrupulously polished table-tops. Candles
began to dislodge from the ceiling. We inspected

the pictures and plaster-casts all around us,
testing their crevices for hidden documents.

Bust after bust we smashed against the walls –
fragments of eyes and noses scattering everywhere
about our heads. After a few hours of this,

we remembered the crowd waiting patiently outside –
it had better have been patient – yes, yes: it was patient –
what reason have you to think they were otherwise? –
and we filed out through the astonishing balcony window.

The others deftly and submissively
motioned me to the microphones at the front.

I protested at this, but I walked forward smoothly enough.

I saw the massed ranks standing in front of me,
most of them far below, or widely distant,
and a surge of pride overtook me. 'Friends!' I cried,

'for I think I may call you friends. Does anyone object?'
(No-one appeared to object.) 'Friends!', I insisted;
'As I look down at you I am inevitably reminded

that somewhere in the terrestrial soil there are earthworms
over twice our average length. Oh, how they must
push push push laboriously through the earth
in a manner familiar to all but the most constipated of us.

Now, everyone to the left of the imaginary
line between my navel (that strange silent testimony
to the fact that all of us must heave our way

into the world of variously running clocks
through an opening which it is possible to call earlike)

between, as I say, my navel and that there
ammonia molecule just caused to vibrate
at 24 billion oscillations per second –

everyone in that segment, without exception,
I order to gasp with ill-concealed wonder at
the size of my private parts. And the rest of you,
go off and invade our neighbours. Go on! Now!'

Then, like the hummingbird, the only avian
capable, to my knowledge, of flying backwards,
I coughed once or twice and watched the clouds descend.

I slip inconspicuously through the corridors of the
distinguished edifice; come round a last
time-honoured corner, and am outside again
in the throbbing street. Or is it me who is throbbing?
Did I plant the device correctly? Or did I,
in a nervous rush of excitement, perhaps forget
to dispose of it at all? But, no: in that case,
I would surely still be walking about with it
in my possession. Yet, what then is this
large strident object which I find in my hands?
No. When I look again, my hands are empty.
So, the mind cools down and returns to other thoughts.
Why, for instance, did I wish to destroy that building?
Think, man; think! You know you had a reason.
And a superb one too! No; it has gone.
I'm afraid for the moment it has gone from me.
I'll remember soon enough. But, whatever it is,
I am sorry that the innocent had to die;
except, of course, that no-one here is really
innocent of the crime, whatever it was.
Anyway; time to turn to other things.
Is it not strange that there are animals which
have not changed, unlike us, within millions of years?
Not the individual organisms, of course –
but that a pair even less separate than
identical twins, can be separated by
not a street, not a moderate length of coast,
not even the traversable ocean; but by
several unsuspected hundreds of thousands
of years – with humdrum living dying and sunlight
at both ends. So, I walk across a street,
smiling an almost entirely reflex smile
at children playing beside a parked car or two.
I fail to drive a car. And, none of these children
is the result of my past exertions, not even
the smallest, whose face is the most evocative.
All wearing clothing bought with so much care,
and such love spread through scattered shops, they participate
in a probably after five years totally

forgotten game – perhaps even in ten minutes.
Suns let their whirling shadows take up space,
let three or four families care for them so painfully;
and I pass into the coolness of the communal
entranceway, for some reason or other.

XVI

I can best describe that latest mood as being
like that bird, which, from sheer joy of living,
appears, falls backwards on its perch, swings round,
and rerights itself on the branch, all the time singing;
though now I sit in this underground beer-cellar,
drinking a local brew which, frankly, I do not like.
Why am I sitting here? I could be elsewhere
(I think I may even claim, I *should* be elsewhere)
otherwise imprinting chance in the biosphere
with more inept gestures and unwitting mistakes –
the whole of which (as I think Monod puts it)
is reflected in the ontogenesis of
a functional protein. A jazz quintet
plays deplorably loudly. Within us all
(I think I may safely make even so broad a claim)
we initiate the creation of new life-forms
on not-yet-populated-by-beings-able-
to-work-out-what-a-planet-might-be planets.
Moderate applause breaks out. Death seems a reasonable
part of existence, like women showing their ears.
Our emptying glasses seem so unworried by
(unlike their ghastlily self-observing drinkers)
the existence of 4000-year-old trees
on another continent. We do not know
if, left to themselves, these plants would ever die;
or if this requires explosives or an earthquake –
survival might simply be their metier,
their forte, the main purpose for which they are here,
or, to be scrupulous, for which they are there –
even though I hold in my cupped palm several million
of the seeds from which such objects grow, and throw them
in immoderate handfuls at the dancing-girls

whenever they stray into good taste. Oh my friend –
if such you are – and be so anyway
till this question ends – when shall we meet again?
For the Empire which we inhabit is vast, and we
are not getting any younger, are we? (China?
Why ask? What difference does it make?) Therefore,
let us drink, not entirely unlike the frog –
even though that cute animal lacks a neck,
which each of us is fortunate enough
to possess. For if it wishes to look somewhere,
it has to turn its whole body! Drink, drink, drink;
let our tongues be like a frog's, which, hinged rather
at the front of the buccal cavity than at the back,
lies inwardly-pointing, like the soul, and able
to leap out like a springed hammer, to crush
some inoffensive insect, even less
popular than ourselves, apparently.

XXVa

I wake up this morning, and at last realise what I must do.
I must entirely conquer the Persian Empire.
Now: where did I put my cigarettes?

*

XXXIV

A pleasant morning. The trees rustle as usual.
If I were alive, is this where I would choose
to be? There is space enough; there is laughter enough.
Even the rooms which are unoccupied
seem, somehow, to be occupied. But, if the chance
had not been missed, what would I have grown into?

Into a fish, perhaps, too stupid to know
it needs to come to the surface of the water
to breathe – which, when it felt the need of air,
drifts towards warmth; and, since the warmer water

94

lies at the surface, manages to survive
until it strays within the power of beings
intelligent enough to provide it with
a tank, artificially heated at
the base! In which case, it sinks to the bottom,
finds its required warmth, and asphyxiates.

Perhaps we are all such fishes anyway.
And could our warm air be love? Find it,
we sink to the bottom and asphyxiate.
But would the asphyxiation then teach us
how over-rated was breathing? What does it matter.

I climbed out of bed, with the strange self-confidence
so typical of the merely potential; took up
the unremarkable, dark blue, ill-used book
from its place on the floor, where I had dropped it, on
the previous evening, and continued reading
a list of the marvels of the animal kingdom,
including, of course, plants. 'Nature', it opined,
'is stranger than fiction.'
                                    Previously, I had
– on preceding days – always agreed with this;
but by now I had frankly lost interest. Who cares
about these prodigies? Only the utterly boring
exist here. A mug casually abandoned
on a table (which ought to have been cleared away,
but wasn't) seems to me in my present mood
far more remarkable than the fact that fish
do not drink water – or, at the very least,
pretend not to. An unhappy, weeping woman,
in the middle of another long grey featureless night,
intermittently masturbating to relieve
the emotional pressure being put upon her,
is far more lovely than the three-toed sloth
hanging upside down from branches, with its fur
a greenish tint thanks to the operation
of symbiotic algae. Even when she stops,
lets her green-coloured nightie slip back down
below her navel, turns over on her stomach,
and begs to be abused with a few branches

which lie scattered about the bedroom, the fact
that a snail is at the partition wall, bending
round the corner its eyes on their long stalks,
and chuckling to itself at our stupidity,
does not impress me as much as her sudden anecdote
about her father. Let the starfish wave
an eye at the end of each of its arms, in seas
which have no conception of dry land; let the ants
enslave 600 other different species
and convince them they are on this earth to benefit
ants; and let her mother – yes, even that
incredible form of life, try to convince her
that she is a fool to put up with the sort of treatment
that I *inflict* on her – what do we care
for the occasional blind passer-by,
we who gather stars each night, exploding, cooling,
condensing, forming, blaring out with incredible
light, plundering the starlit sky, until it
is almost as dark, almost as mysterious,
almost as deep, almost as promising,
and almost as impossible as that there.
Oh, you do not see it; but I see it.
I see it. I see it. I see it. I see it. I see it.

from *Everything is Strange*
(1994)

from *Last Eternal Moments*

1
No, thanks. I'd rather have another Universe.
Something a little brighter, if you don't mind.

2
Blood is another object not impossible in the universe;
As is a red dress, draped over the back of a chair.
What a huge sound a cup makes, knocking against a saucer!

4
Throw your toys onto the floor.
Abandon your game spectacularly,
And put on exquisite adult clothing.
Move about my room with a rare grace,
Accustomed by now, I suppose, to being a woman.
After all, we must learn the truth some time.
And if we do not learn the truth some time,
We shall die without ever learning it, I suppose.

5
Meanwhile, the duck, which once thought whatever it thought,
Before a Chinese cook so expertly treated its carcass,
Will very soon be adding to the pulsing chaos
Of the numerous progeny of our interiors.
Hordes die every second, unsuspected, in our bloodstreams;

Millions of them. Millions. Millions. And not only in the bloodstream.
Your eyes sparkle. Are my eyes sparkling too?
Children must be sleeping not very far from here.

6
Another morning. More people with dangling penises
Are killing each other in the name of infinite powers.
I'll probably go to the library again this afternoon.

12
Thanks to an explosion perhaps eight billion years ago,
We hurry towards a train; and we catch it just in time.
How surprised they will surely be to see us this afternoon!
(Not unreasonably so, under the circumstances.)

13
Truly, in the four-fifths of an eternity
in which hydrogen, its derivatives and its predecessors
have whistled outwards, combining and recombining;
in the billions of years in which chaotic gases and liquids
gave the earth innumerable unseen surfaces;
in the unimaginable tempests of the unimportant sun;
in the slow drift of unsuspected vibrant species to land;
in the huge rock-crystals that hurl negligently past nearby;
in the tiny crystals which can change us utterly;
in the inextinguishable heat which shrieks and rampages
somewhere away beneath that most elegant footwear
discarded beside a bed, upon which a woman
lies, laughing, as she reads out something absurd from a magazine –
so devastating a complex pattern of simple sounds –
that this shy hill, whose crest we help to populate
is instantly revealed to be the living centre
of Time and History and Joy and Musicality –
and Something Else even greater – what is it called?
Oh, keep talking; keep talking until I can remember.
Another four-fifths of a second should be all I need.

15
What did they want? What did they think they wanted?
They are all dead. What would they have preferred?
Were they fairly treated? Did they cry for a long time?
If so, how far away are they now in the sky?

If not, how far away are they in the sky now?
But what sky is there, except this same sky here?
And I could lie in your garden, watching these clouds
For longer, longer, and longer. Such special clouds
To float so directly above your abandoned towel.

16

The day after the last day will be of quite staggering beauty.
Rather like the whole universe waking up in your bed;
To find itself looking at an imitation antique clock
Which you must surely have chosen for yourself.
Will loud footsteps also be disappearing on the nearest street?

18

The sound of a father playing gleefully with his daughter –
Or is that his son? I cannot be quite sure –
Reverberates noisily through my dull beige ceiling
From the room directly above. Only now,
Having stopped reading, do I become aware of it.
I put down on the table a book purchased last week,
In which, among so many Chinese details,
In rain falling more than a thousand years ago,
A man is glancingly reminded of his native village.

19

A fairly normal day – the tall gent in Room 6
is playing rubbishy music with his habitual loudness;
so that the monotonous repetitive drumbeats
win their way through, maddeningly, into my own abode.
And, turning from one form of penetration to another,
through the wall to my left, the modest elderly couple
who make occasional appearances during the daylight hours
on a principle which I cannot even surmise,
are now, to judge from a usual repertoire
of sighs and grunts, heading for the ultimate bliss.
The bright cold light contains the voices of children
shouting in a nearby school – where, thirty years ago,
I too was a pupil, now sitting as I am
in front of a gas-fire; somewhat disappointed
to have yet again received no letters today,
and leafing desultorily through a book about free will.

21

Another morning, and letters continue to scurry
over most of the globe, in terrifying profusion;
over-compensating for the doubtless soon to be resumed
millennia of utter terrestrial letterlessness.
Odd, all this communication in the vast dark.
That I lay awake for so much of last night
now seems to have been rendered hideously irrelevant –
thinking and rethinking of one particular woman's actions,
torturingly intermingled with her inactions,
who once again this morning has not yet written to me,
perhaps to tell me how she might once more be reached,
or at least to enclose some helpful, discarded underwear.
However, even now her letters might be travelling
to unknown destinations and their fortunate recipients;
possibly at the other end of the earth;
possibly to a near neighbour in this street.
I read my latest postcard from Switzerland anyway,
and, within ten minutes of receiving it,
I pin it to the normal wall. There it shall stay
for the next few dozen days, so I suppose,
through morning after morning of lengthening silence.
Eventually, the silence will prove to be unbreakable.

22

Can't someone force time, or merely the world, to behave properly?
You kiss a woman's ——, and she then marries someone else!
That may even have been her you passed in a busy lane this evening.

23

Very well, my darling, let me answer your question seriously,
Since you persist with it in that unignorable voice.
I shall leave brilliance to more appropriate occasions.
As I find myself doing more and more often nowadays.
No. I do not wonder who else I might have been, if not me.
Those who were not conceived are not non-existent people.
They are not even 'those who were never conceived'.
They are nothing. There is no such they in existence.
At most they are possibilities which exist, or once existed,
In more than one object scattered throughout real space.
You are puzzled that I so love certain photographs.

But all the ingredients needed for photography
Existed long before photography itself appeared.
The dispersed ingredients are not the thing itself.
The incipient human being, likewise, arrives only at conception.
Before that, there are only possible constitutents,
Variously disposable within different agencies.
How else, anyway, *ought* we to be elaborated?
A characterless sperm outstrips such millions of others,
And gets so subtly to a tiny point first; even though
Still you are nowhere, even you, until that initial impact,
And so strange a presence directly after that moment.
But look: we have somehow developed beyond that moment.
We may possibly face each other across a table,
A table resplendent with china, light and newspapers;
And that we emerged from infinitesimal, intricate tubes
Should be accepted as true; for, amazingly, it *is* true.
After all: where else is love supposed to emerge from?
What other way ought there to be of producing it?
For our emotions must develop from real physical objects,
However subtle they grow, however rich, however all-pervasive,
Unless we are to be satisfied with merely imaginary love.
And my love for you is not an imaginary love.

25
This is already the other world that you are in.
Any cloud could tell you that, if you watched it properly.

26
And so the nymph, waiting patiently at the taxi-rank,
Eager to take to a desperate person waiting for them
Kindness, understanding, various adorable
Orifices, and possibly even love –
Irritated by the relentless braying fatuity
Of a loud person next to her in the queue,
Silenced him with an expert flick of her wrist,
And suavely addressed him thus. Oh, very well.
Very well. Let me try again, since you insist.
It is not inapt that I should have to repeat myself
As far as I can. The point bears repetition.
All the same, it surprises me that you should find so elusive
The thought that any real thing must be one particular thing.

That particular thing, and not any other.
For nothing, whatever it is, is actually something else;
Not if we are talking of real, existing objects.
And insofar as anything is a particular thing,
By that very fact it cannot be made twice.
Two distinct examples of it simply cannot occur,
Any more than the same life can have two separate mid-points.
However similar one point may be to another,
You cannot have two instances of the one particular point.
Let me try to extend the point a little further.
Whichever was the process which made a particular thing,
Exactly the same process cannot repeat itself,
For the repetition of something is not the thing itself.
Even the repetition of the same act
Is not the same act as the same act it repeats;
For the second is a repetition, and the first is not.
Let me try to extend the point a little further.
After the extinction of life in your own body,
You cannot come back to life as the same person,
For the person in question has actually ceased to exist.
Nor can you come back after death as somebody else.
Only someone else can appear. And someone else,
It should hardly need to be said, will not be you.
Even the reconstitution of your own body –
Whatever feasible process such a phrase could possibly indicate –
Would provide only a replica of your body;
And a replica of a thing is not the thing itself.
I concede that this argument is none too original.
Lucretius pointed most of it out millennia ago.
But numerous different minds, combining into existence,
Then uncombining back into non-existence,
To provide the raw material for some other things –
Now that their interlude of puzzlement is over –
Have missed this rather simple point in century after century after
     century.

27
Morning. The clock is almost screaming with happiness.
God has evidently locked Himself into the bathroom with you.
Three inviting letters wait on the table to be opened.

28

A morning like this surely gives me the right to invoke them –
If anything does. All those people who were never created!
All those possibilities who were never realised!
Even though, of course, there cannot be such people –
What fascinating remarks would fill their treasured childhoods.
What stabs would hit them as unknown others entered a room.
What furtive, regretted acts they might even have committed.
And what children they too might have managed to produce;
Whom they would sit beside in kitchens very like this,
Planting warm, cautious kisses on those frail, somehow real skulls,
As a voice from the nearby television talked about coming storms.

29

We are (I hope) all familiar with that calmness
when the pain of a dental injection has at last
disappeared, as one always knew it would, yet somehow
never quite believed beforehand; and one no longer
touches the sore place with one's tongue, trying to gauge
how much more time must pass before the face
recovers the normal feeling of a normal face,
which is what, apparently, it used to have. In the next space,
if the recent, cryptic remark which she made in passing
is, as we say here, anything to go by,
and I have interpreted it correctly, someone
of inexpressible beauty is doing something
alas inexpressible in another way.
After she had left, noticing my calming jaw,
I picked up the pen on the table, and began writing
impromptu on the back of a defunct sheet of paper
of the sort which the bank seems to think itself qualified
to address to her. And I find that my thoughts turn,
as they so often seem to do nowadays,
to thoughts of extinction; which I find a fashionable –
albeit perhaps a merely transient fashion –
and genuinely interesting subject. For, although
if we don't all disappear now, we shall all disappear later,
whether tomorrow or in sixty years' time;
and our artworks will anyway wholly evaporate,
like the once so plentiful excrement of any number
of eliminated beasts; on perhaps a

correspondingly large number of planetary
surfaces; we would still prefer to wait a little,
by and large. So every pregnant woman
appears to possess a heartening faith in the future,
and the neighbours' children, when depression looms,
become, though scarcely likeable, yet at least
useful little loud bad-tempered arguments.
They suggest that things will continue; and she will return.
Not before time, I may add. Still absent. Still absent.

30

Out on a walk along Great Western Road,
I toss a letter I have carried too far in my pocket
Into a sudden pillar box which I have never used before.
I have passed by it a few times in my forty years, I suppose.
Two days later, I get an answer from Dundee –
A city which I do not remember ever visiting.

33

The sound of a plane fades away over the roof opposite.
Half an hour since the voice on the telephone
Told me of my aunt's death. I stand at a window.
In one of the lit rooms visible across the lane
Two adults and two children are sitting round a table,
Their gestures so lively in the renewed silence.
What noise they must be making, from the look of things.

34

That the East has produced much of value hardly needs to be said.
But I doubt whether all its mystic wisdom put together
Is as miraculous as the very material workings of the telephone.
A slight noise, then devastating warm tones from a distance.

35

The slow movement of the Mozart two-piano sonata
continues to issue from the stereo cassette-deck,
which has a slight imbalance between its speakers –
the left being privileged – as I look up
from a not particularly good book about Zen
by someone called Eugen Herrigel, realising
that my father and mother, at present in the small

and not overwhelmingly famous town of East Kilbride,
southwards along the coast, are both still alive,
and merely doing some shopping. Somehow this seems
an almost unbearable success. A light breeze disorders
the treelet (whose genus I must try to find out)
in the brief garden beside the road, and I
reflect for a moment about how little I know
of my father's complex and baffling itinerary
during the last war, over four decades ago;
deciding that the details will probably escape me
forever, as I glance down again to relocate
some moderately interesting remarks about Japanese acting.

36
Having switched the lamp off at night in the large low attic
Of my parents' house, I turn back to the pillow,
And almost at once grow aware of a brightness
Curiously enveloping me. My alerted eyes
Seek out the small skylight somewhere beyond my head;
And there, caught so neatly, hangs a huge full moon.
So much light, so much light; such a ridiculous amount of light
To be propagated across a near-empty near-infinity,
Through oceans of fine dust, to be intercepted
Somewhere halfway along a modestly important road
In a not particularly important town on a coastline.
I maintain my ever more locked gaze, until
It seems it is simply a lack of confidence prevents me
From reaching out slowly into the narrow darkness
As if to an elegant, sleeping face nearby,
And touching an utterly distant forehead for reassurance.
However, time will pass, and one falls asleep
Whether beside live foreheads or dead planets,
And mornings eventually follow of widely different characters.
In these, one may very well be extremely alone.
Or the door of the room directly underneath may open,
While various parents casually emerge from it,
Adding normal words to an already normal morning.

37
The mind cannot encompass all the important silences at once.
Newer vacancies jostle against so many of their predecessors.

Other pleasant breakfasts are no doubt being prepared
Elsewhere than in this friendly, agreeable kitchen,
Where I sit talking to a very close relative,
Our words interspersed with long, amiable silences.
But even to be surrounded by voices which one loves
Is not always to be surrounded by the right voices.
There are still necessary and desired elsewheres being occupied,
Where the wrong clocks agree to signal the correct time,
While the wrong mail drops through the nearby letterbox.

38

Between one heartbeat and another, what disappears?
Something usually too insignificant to notice.
To wit, the entire previous state of the Universe.

39

Smoke floating above the sea, as if it were
A more leisurely sort of bird. A sort of bird
Not quite realised in the wheeling forms
Which, on our roofs, make such unattractive noises.
We waken up, and the smoke of dreams drifts out
Into the bright neat room, as if it were
Only a sharpness which the air takes on
In yet another ordinary morning.

40

Each dawn need not happen. But it does.
And when it doesn't, something else happens instead.

43

After much trouble in a complexity
Of corridors and stairways, the nymph at last
Locates the City Architect's Office, enters,
Crosses to where the relevant functionary is slumped,
Thoughtful, behind a desk. She sits down opposite,
Pulls out a notebook, and refreshes her memory.
The traffic flowing outside pretends to ignore her.
She smiles at a passing, silent thought. Then, crossing
Her sacred legs, without further preliminary,
She launches into the following genuine interrogation:
The buildings where we were born were never built, were they?

They were never mere plans, or merely half-constructed.
It seems they were always there. Always already there.
And, since we are much the same, that is surely appropriate.
Manufactures of impeccable timelessness,
We walk through them, or drift ethereally out of them.
We were not produced in any way at all, were we,
As the result of the somewhat crass activity
Of some probably not too well-known gent's penis. Were we?
With whom, perhaps, we long afterwards argued.
Or never saw. Or received superb advice from –
Possibly concerning the nature of the other sex.
Oh dear, no. Nothing as realistic as that.
That sort of crude materialism is not applicable to *us*,
Off whom the light reflects as clinically
As it does from the music-producing equipment beside us;
Below the piles of books by major philosophers,
Perhaps, produced by bloodless thinking machines.
Nothing to do with the seepage of fluids here.
Vaginas? Well, they are all very pretty, no doubt;
But one wouldn't exactly choose to be born from one, would one?
All far too blood-stained and undignified
For creatures of such immense spiritual sophistication;
So intent on grasping and transmuting the universe
Till it glows with a perfect, immaterial illumination.
But how do things look in the actual light? That is the first question.

45

It is not really happening – I am not really
Walking down this street, caught precariously
In a crossfire of sunlight and wind, towards
A relative whom I have not seen for years.
I am not quite waiting for these traffic-lights to change,
And the members of the crowd who break past me
On either side, with such odd resolution,
Are not quite in the thoughts of unseen, breathing figures.

47

How can you argue seriously with some whose c—— you have touched?
What strange routes we have come down to reach this public anger.
Can she really talk to her parents in the same tone of voice sometimes?

48

I see the main street has its usual crowd this morning.
I suppose I am forced to conclude it is only another real morning.
I suppose I may even buy another newspaper soon,
And read it as one reads an ordinary newspaper;
More struck than usual, perhaps, by the strange ill-timing
With which others vanish, through accident or age,
Having gathered together their full heaps of futile, irrelevant years.
By now, she must have entered the building where she works,
With that soft perfect skin transcendently dry and unmarked.
But who are all these people standing so unconcerned near me?
If I gave a shriek of joy, would they even hear me?
We stand, all separately waiting at the same lights.

51

What numerous rooms I have caught myself saying your name in!
I have scattered it for many months throughout various cities,
And throughout numerous districts of the same city.
You too must have been in some of them, I suppose;
But never exactly in one of those exact places.
Not that callously ugly garden near a skyscraper;
Not that rich beautiful street full of blondes and sportscars;
Not that friend's dull kitchen, in some desperate moment
Of a needless morning, alone. Not here; not now.
Always you have been elsewhere, saying whatever you are saying;
Addressing whatever people you are addressing
By whatever names you choose to address them by.
Then they will often use your own name in reply.

54

All deeds produce results, and most absences of deeds too.
I am sitting alone in this room because of real and unreal telephone calls.
In other rooms move the hands that I should be catching by the wrist.

58

Curious, the precision of this foreign country.
The ranks of newspapers outside its sunlit kiosks.
People who stand, exchanging the wrong consonants,
Then move off suddenly down different streets.
Let us follow any one – this one, for instance.
Let us follow him down this street, and up this stairway.

Let us watch him take a key out of his pocket,
Open the door with great ease, and go through
Into a house with which he is perfectly familiar.
Let us hurry out of a nearby kitchen to greet him,
Our beautiful face combining thoughtfulness and chic.
He plants a benign, somewhat absent kiss on this cheek;
Then goes off into his study, unfolding a newspaper.

59

Through the neighbouring wall, the sounds of two voices reach me.
One of them is a visitor's; the other, my mother's.
I smile, fold over the newspaper, and continue to read.

61

A charming soft low voice crept up behind me,
And whispered: do you mind if I ask you a personal question?
Why is it so insulting to be only a part
Of a real, limited universe? What else could anything be?
Anything which is the product of real objects and events
Must be the product of in some way limited objects and events.
How else can one be acted on, but by circumstances
Which actually exist? Which are this rather than that;
Lying one way rather than all ways; slow rather than fast;
Or fast rather than slow; hot rather than cold;
Music rather than silence; oxygen rather than gold.
Listen: anything real is composed of actual details.
A particular composition of particular details.
Why this vast, abiding shame about the actual world?
The Universe is shunned like a guilty family secret.
But anything real must be part of something real –
Unless it is in fact everything. And few of us,
For all our inbuilt positional megalomania,
Are prepared to go quite as far, in a literal sense, as that.
So the people we meet cannot help but be the people
From that part of the universe we are travelling through.
For, if they were not, how could we ever meet them?
What other sort of being could anyone ever meet?
Perfect, unlocated, transcendental automorphs,
Wholly devoid of circumstantial detail,
Do not and cannot exist. Where could they be?
It would flout their composition to be actually anywhere.

It would not be good enough, even if it were possible,
To be manufactured outside the Universe –
Which is to say, surely, outside of everywhere –
Then squeezed in wherever appropriate, as if
The cosmos were a sort of large box with a hole in it,
Which life, or something else, could be forced in through from outside.
At which point the nymph stopped talking. She blushed deeply,
Gave a brief curse, then rushed out into the hallway,
Letting an incomparable silence descend on the small room
Which only the newborn child – but enough of this for the moment.

62

Merely because something of infinite value is now so near,
And we do not nearly understand how it can be so near;
Emerged at length from such a tangle of possibilities
Which the understanding loses itself in seeking to follow;
The remote galaxies have not become less numerous,
Nor the objects which may be bigger than the galaxies,
Whether remoter or imperfectly realised by us,
Who, after all, fail to realise so much,
Even this inexhaustible small world before our eyes.
Certainly, the unbelievable astronomy books
Remain on sale in the shops, and on view in the libraries.
Each of our discoveries would surely dwarf us further
If size were the same thing as significance.
But, if size were the same thing as significance,
Why would that tiny object dressed in miniature clothes,
Clothes that hardly seem bigger than the idea of clothes;
Why would that small object, which you hold in your arms,
That tiny object, lost in its own dreams,
Not yet knowing whose body it is clutched against,
Whose beautiful, enchanted, productive body;
Why would the least, sudden, gratuitous shift of its head,
Which it can move through such impossible distances,
Such vast, spasmodic, untrackable distances,
Thrown out from next to nothing, into such distances
Which can somehow be contained in this normal room,
This normal room in a city full of rooms?

63

What? Were you really once a child, really and truly?
Show me the entire universe in a half-filled blue cup.
Like that cup on the table beside your ten-year-old hand,
In a photograph which your adult hand now reaches out towards me.

65

Though once you pushed, pushed, desperately pushed;
And a child's head painfully, unbelievably emerged –
Two years on, you talk to me gaily outside a bank –
In this street full of talking, alert heads –
The child, I suppose, yawning in a room somewhere nearby –

66

Oh, what is not contained here in this small room!
Just kick the Sombrero Galaxy behind that chair.
Or whatever it is. One of your dropped shoes?
Let me put back in the drawer underneath the window
This object here – what is it? A useless knife,
Or perhaps the History of the Development of Thought.
It is clearly one or the other. What is that noise?
Have you reinvented the lost music of the Greeks,
Or are you asking me about the evening meal?
Oh, the scent of European Civilization –
Perhaps even more! – drifts in from the kitchen.
If I could only purée the entire Universe,
It might just yield the proper adjective for what we now feel,
Wrestling with God or the too tight lid of a pickle-jar,
While Eternity lightly wrinkles her glorious troubled eyebrows.

67

I follow you nonchalantly past a lightly opened doorway.
What a huge, astonishing sight I glimpse on the other side.
Is the Andromeda Galaxy really bigger than your bed?
I suppose it must be. How terribly impressive.
Was someone really asleep there a few bare hours ago?

68

A trio of youths outside a shop mock the shape of my beard.
Their cruel laughter reaches upwards into the air, and vanishes.
The air extends further, until it too vanishes.
Soon there is only the darkness of space, with occasional little dots in it.

70

Ah! The long mute emptiness of space is broken here –
Or, at least, it was here only a minute ago –
By a vast, rotating, slowly dripped together pebble.
And, for a few seconds in its day or so of existence,
On odd, largely silent, non-liquid bits of its volume,
Quaint bipeds inhale and exhale various gases
Without particularly noticing that they are doing so.
Some of which are disagreements about why they might be there;
Some of which are unequalled declarations of love;
Some of which are are thrilling political shrieks;
Some of which are mature, gnomic shafts of understanding;
Some of which are infinitesimal hidden sighs,
Emitted for an unknown reason during sleep
By someone whose near silent head moves and moves,
Visible in the dim light of a digital clock,
Operating in a manner which I do not quite grasp –

71

On how many nights have you lain beside that man?
I lie awake, torturing myself by my own imagination.
I could ask myself, what are you doing, in a house not far from here.
I struggle not to think of what it is you might be doing.
Let me think of nothing but sleep. Nothing but sleep.
Your sleep. His sleep. No: even that is too much.
How can the Universe let you lie asleep beside someone else?
Why does it not intervene, spontaneously,
To correct this so obviously idiotic arrangement?
I could switch on a light, and look at a red curtain;
The back of a chair, a picture of a cup;
Even, in the tiny distance, a photograph of you.
Yet someone else, not twenty streets from here,
Could turn on a light and see that face itself.
What emotion do you think this is? Guess anyway.
Or am I the only one who must guess such things?

72

Such an enchanting semblance of compassion
Was the late beautiful light among the autumnal trees,
Casting leafy shadows onto its playing children
Like a loving warm relative, anxious to protect them;

While their mothers stand in the street, talking in clear tones,
And letting their legs be admired with great subtlety.
Oh, clearly, there is nothing that belongs here more than we do.
Yet, what does any star really care whether it is shining
On 13 lifeless planetoids, or merely upon 12?
Is the 13th also there, not yet devoid of life?
Are there philosophers on it, trying to devise
Proper rules for conduct? Are there numerous bodies
Being slaughtered or merely coerced in tribute to
Dazzlingly imaginary Gods? Are its grandmothers
Gazing tearfully at brand-new precarious children?
Are there people sniffing in untidy sunlit rooms
As they jot down brief remarks about possibilities of lifelessness?
Here? There? Where? What does it matter?
Nothing matters more, of course – but what does it matter?
And if it mattered more, what would that too matter?
Some worry that the world may possibly have no point.
Others are drawn to a somewhat intenser question:
What could possibly be the point of having a point?

73
Very well. It will soon be time to leave.
Your father walks pensively across the room,
A wise, tense man with a lifetime's experience;
By now, I would guess, incapable of breaking into a run.
You derive in part from a transient shiver of his body.
Even those priceless legs, which still may run when they need to.
The least grain in his coffee-cup is bigger than what you once were.
Or what he once was, if it comes to that. Or me too.
Oh, these teasing, unoriginal thoughts about origins!
Some male approaching some female, not so long ago,
(Or let it be her approaching him, if you prefer;
The exact sequence of moves is not the point at issue),
And you still nowhere; or me; or whoever it is –
Except that no 'whoever it is' is there yet;
Only so many possibilities distributed
In tiny particles ascending or descending
The adjacent coils of intricate interiors
In a manner rather too hard to contemplate.
For the thought of one's father's —— in an excited state
Is not something one likes to dwell upon,

However nearly one once dwelt within it.
In fact, so unattractive is such a prospect
That most, I suppose, never face the thought at all.
Where you are concerned, there is even less seductiveness.
To think of him approaching some smiling woman,
And you still nowhere, even when the caresses start!
Odd, to have so much difficulty in coping with
What one cannot even begin to deny was necessary.
Odd, but for human beings a remarkably common state.
Odd too, to watch your father come into the room,
Talking to you nonchalantly about air-travel,
As if all of us had always been this size,
This habitual weight and bulk and spaciousness,
Rather than, say, each tinier than your ——,
That priceless central detail, so easily overlooked,
Which somehow he was able to help have developed,
From a roughly equivalent structure now utterly absent,
So that, a filling slice of a century later,
A complete stranger, from a wholly different place –
(After much thought, I remove a dozen or so lines.)

74
Is there always another child perhaps; the child you did not have?
The third child, perhaps, of the family with two?
The second child, likewise, of the family with one?
The only child of the childless couple, who find better things to do?
Or perhaps they are mute and devastated by its absence.
The planet spins on its way, anyway, slightly flattened at the poles.
So many schools release so many children each day,
But even from there, so near the moon, no-one hears their shouting.
No-one can see in which room in the same street
A childless person sits at a table writing,
Not far away from a picture of colossal stellar clouds;
While a neighbour helps a child with mathematics homework:
Aid being given to someone else who has also, somehow, arrived.
But by now the planet has moved slightly further, still flattened at the
        poles.

76
Some think God tortures us because he loves us so much.
What a shame he does not hate us, and treat us kindly.

Thus: every evening, regularly, for six or seven years,
The inoffensive and devout middle-aged woman
Lights a candle in front of a favoured religious image,
And prays intently. I do not know what for,
But it was not for this. One night, the candle
Catches the hem of her highly flammable nightdress,
Envelops her in flames, and burns her to death.
Thus she is taken off to meet her God of Love,
Possibly with a ready question on her lips.
Let us hope he was wearing some means of identification.
He could so easily be mistaken for his opposite number
By anyone who judges character in the light of actions.

77
What we disappear into is neither light nor darkness.
What we disappear into is merely disappearance.

78
Look. This here is the Universe. There is nothing behind it.
Nor is there anything in front of it.
The great trembling secret behind all existing things
Is only the existence of existence itself.
It is not something else, existing behind existence.
Behind existence, there is only non-existence,
Which is also in front of it, and on either side of it –
Or would be, if it existed. Which it does not.
That which seems to lie behind all religions,
Making them sound vaguely some chord of a great music,
Is merely the actual existence of life itself.
It is exactly the same thing that lies behind everything else.
Anything additional is more or less imaginary.
No single vast cosmic force unites all religions.
If one did, no doubt it would be human gullibility –
Unless we prefer the claims of megalomania.
Our Gods are our own echoes mistaken for other voices.
Each believer misinterprets in his own way the silence of heaven.
For we are producing voices in the skies,
Who were ourselves produced by the actions of the skies;
And to mistake chance noises for a voice
Undervalues the rarity of real, undeniable voices.
Oh, when shall I ever hear your glorious real voice again?

Yes, yes. It emerged from an infinity of unlikelihoods,
But the very next call this morning on the telephone,
That calm, miraculous object which clings to the wall of the hallway,
That Mozart of limpets, could bring it back to me –
Or traces of it sufficient to reassure me
That the disposition of matter in the Universe
Still balances in its present apotheosis.

80

In a quiet afternoon, on the seventh floor of the library,
Among the numerous long rows of undisturbed volumes
Devoted to various aspects of religion and philosophy,
I caught sight of the nymph. She was in the next bay,
Elegantly disfiguring selected clamant textbooks
With charming little diagrams, most of them obscene.
What are you doing, I asked her, shocked to the core –
For I knew the answer at once. Do you not understand
That such behaviour could seriously compromise
Your status as a ticket-holder? Those warning placards
Attached to the walls and doorways leave little doubt of this.
She finished drawing a neat, intricate vulva
On a book about a great religious leader
(The second greatest ever produced, perhaps);
Replaced it, thus enhanced, on the shelves; looked round;
Gazed deep into my eyes; then slightly deeper –
And spoke as follows in a warm, melodious,
Deeply convincing voice. Listen, my overweight friend.
For millions upon millions upon millions of years the dinosaurs ——.
As did any number of defunct genera before and after.
A stratospherically exact number of such occasions
Available to the assiduous, omniscient researcher.
And every one of our great religions was still in the future –
Which is to say, nowhere – for the future is nowhere, as is
The diarrhoea which the plums will cause, before the plums are eaten.
For billions of years, no terrestrial had need of them.
How curious, then, that none of your great religions
Is more than .0002% of the age of the earth.
And none, I dare say, of our non-great religions either.
It shows you just how misleading statistics can be, doesn't it?
Here: this morning's newspaper provides further examples
Of the inexhaustible riches of Man's spiritual heritage.

116

Another few dozen, it seems, have been killed in that Indian town
Where a deity was once born in the form of an elephant.
Or was it a monkey? It was a monkey, I think.
Yes; the more I consider it, the more a monkey convinces me.
It has a pleasantly pseudo–Darwinian ring about it.
Perhaps another God was born nearby as a barrel-organ.
(For who are we to assign limits to his powers?)
I would suppose that, if God is to appear anywhere,
The most obvious place to do it would be China.
That China wasn't chosen seems itself sufficiently damning:
Our largest civilisation is there, waiting for him.
That would surely be the most predictable place to start.
Perhaps it goes against the grain to be so predictable?
Or perhaps, on second thought, he had little choice,
Given his unfortunate opinion of the pig,
But avoid a country where porkers are ubiquitous.
How thoughtful of God, to give us his opinion of the pig.
Which of us is not, after all, allergic to something or other?
But what a pity he failed to be equally specific
About some more contentious, metaphysical questions
Which have been argued over for year after year after year,
And not infrequently killed for. As far as I understand it,
We may cull this mighty lesson from many profound religions:
God has revealed innumerable vital truths to us;
But no-one can say for certain exactly what they are.
And now, if you don't mind, I'll take off my underpants.

81
Of course, one may find wisdom even in sacred books.
Just as, for instance, one may find a stray banknote inside one.
Neither, however, is something one can depend on.

85
God creates sinners, and then punishes them for their sins.
I suspect the Devil rather wishes he had thought of that one first.

89
The Universe is wholly uninterested in applause.
Whenever applause stops, it has to continue anyway.

91

A tentative golden light is caught by the window.
We hear a few details of an infinite story
Which has been spreading everywhere for billions of years.
We are given a few details to work upon;
And the strange thing is, we change it utterly.
We are smaller than one full-stop in any of these books
In this room which contains too many trivial books.
All our known universe is perhaps less than that chair.
Can I even begin to estimate how long I have had that chair?
The back is slightly broken, and I well remember
Already being bored with it five or six years ago.
How tensely she has gathered herself, a transient at its edge!
She moves her arms gently, to avoid alarming the cosmos.
And seeing the elegant watch lie so neatly on her wrist,
I find I am getting jealous even of Time itself:
An abstraction which some would claim does not even exist;
A mere interrelationship of objects which do exist.
Yet more torture at the thought of an imaginary rival!

94

Which of our great-great-grandmothers is that,
Swaying inflammatorily down a narrow passageway,
Dazzlingly naked but for neat little boots,
To taunt a man who has seen three continents?
None of them? Are you sure? Are you quite sure?
How easily her progeny loses contact!
Why then does the man who is looking at her buttocks,
Barely able to suppress a scream of triumph,
Wipe away a tear as he thinks of Japanese arbours?
Please do not say: nobody knows any more.
Not even if he is thinking of Japanese harbours?
Will no-one ever again turn the handle of that door?
Oh, all that planning in demolished buildings!
All that planning for what? Was it for this?
For me to watch that postcard near the window of your kitchen
Quiver a little in the surprisingly fresh breeze…

97

It is difficult not to feel that, in some sense, health
is wasted on the healthy; ten minutes after

one has, in a strange town, encountered someone
whom one knows – someone, that is to say,
whom one has met and talked to several times before.
Her bicycle has disappeared over an exultant hill,
and now one is walking through an avenue of trees
where one used to meet one's sister, in those months
when her presence graced this town; swelling its population
for a moment as brief as the turning of that car-wheel;
and that car-wheel; and that car-wheel; though what country
they come from I do not know. However, glancing upwards,
I notice, at a window of one of the preconstructed
sheds sitting in the grounds of the Infirmary,
on top of another such shed, three nurses' heads,
all wearing uniform bonnets, and all laughing.
The leafy sunlight is joining in their joke.

98
Such rain; such wind; such further rain;
Such further rain; only the schoolchildren
Released for their dinner hour, seem not to notice it.
Slightly downhill, the chunky, highish church
Looks solider than ever; but how drenched
Its noble slabs are, glowing wetly,
Brilliantly, morosely, high up over the street.
And the ornate empty niches also, that decorate
The changing angles of the spire, seem now
Too frail to withstand one more assault like that just past.
Too strong a wind whips between their pillars.
The holy stone effigies are no longer there
On their high stone pedestals. Were they ever in place?
Or were they perhaps plucked out by passing waves,
Crashing to the ground, headfirst, on unseen sidestreets?
If so, for what reason? What would be adequate?
Clearly, that you have just passed! They lie in clusters
Of shattered stone, but joyfully, on those streets
Which the last day or so has heard you use;
Or they cling to the stonework near those windows which
You have recently looked out of. Cross to a window!
Gaze out! If it were really happening,
What shrieks, what cries of joy you would surely hear!
The fragments dance dizzily in the shocked city.

They leap joyfully down. They surmount the ridges
That make informal horizons in city streets.
Oh, long rows of the staggeringly bemused!
You pity them do you not? Or would you not?
Do tears perhaps fill your perfect neighbouring eyes,
As you look up in your centrally heated apartment,
Hearing the brave chorus of their distant, cracked voices
Disappear down the road beyond as they sing you
Their unutterably beautiful serenade, beginning
(For how else ought one to serenade the unutterably beautiful?):
'Try to be good, and try to expect nothing.
However, if you do receive anything, try to be grateful.'

101

Morning runs along at your neat heels, shivering joyfully.
The future is continuing to plant its tiny, glorious seeds.
Lie for another fifteenth of a second on your bed.
The whole world will collapse and die of joy if you move too soon.
Please, please do not provoke it. Let it wait till you are gone.

102

So much nonsense about love duping us
Would only make sense if we did not belong
To these present circumstances; to this place and time –
As if we had merely floated in by mistake
From non-existence, and a wrong shrewd universe
Had glued us to the spot. Whatever depths
We find in each other's presence are real depths.
We are not measuring a world with the wrong tools.
Since no-one guides the world, we are not his fools;
Not brainless, storm-tossed, sub-sub-subdivisions.
We are here, and it is up to us to decide.
And whatever we decide, they are real decisions.
Let us leave unreality to the unreal.

105

Leaving the Book Festival for a brief break
between the various famous authors discussing imagination
and the evening session, when other famous authors
will discuss – what is it? – something else, to enjoy
on my own responsibility some of what remains

of a wonderful sunlit afternoon, I wander about
noncommittally at first, finding myself
trailing for no sure reason down Queensferry Street,
over cobbles and past a truly remarkable staircase,
following various noisy youths, who providentially
disappear somewhere while I am investigating
doorways, windows, houses, cars and paving-stones.
I start to cross a bridge, a magnificent high bridge
soaring above a barely discernible waterway,
beyond which might have been built a regal crescent
on the crown of a tree-lined hill. The houses are there,
but they face away; with delightful self-assurance
showing only their mighty, uncaring backs to the vista
in a gesture, I hope, more of indifference than contempt.
While down below, half masked by all those trees,
there appears to be a sort of public garden,
beautifully tended and sparsely occupied.
In it, far off, a woman lies on her back,
in summery clothes, holding a baby. She lifts it
high above her, to the full extent of her arms,
shaking it. Despite the distance, the height, the traffic,
and the fact that she is ninety per cent inference,
it is perfectly clear to me that she is laughing.
Five seconds in the air; ten seconds in the air;
then brought back down to rest upon her body.
It seems I can even hear the child laughing too.
Such is the joy we may give to total strangers.

106 *Joy*
My mother beats the wall, letting me know that breakfast is ready –
while I stand, reading about some Byzantine emperors.
Unhurriedly, I go through to collect my plate.

from *In a Persian Garden*

35

All wrong; all wrong. All in the end are wrong.
No-one hears all the music of the song.
A few notes here are caught; a few notes there.
But even these few notes none can hold for long.

69

Passionate particles of dust and sun,
Run your brief race, nor ask why it is run –
We are all shadow-pictures, voices, dreams.
Perhaps for purposes; perhaps for fun.

95

We ask and ask; and where real questions lie
We may succeed, or fail, before we die;
But All-That-Is is not a question – more
A statement. How then are we to reply?

96

Passionate particles of dust and sun,
Run your brief race, for races should be run.
If we are only shadows, voices, dreams –
Whose are the purposes? Whose is the fun?

99

Of all my seeking this is all my gain:
No agony of any mortal brain
Shall wrest a secret of the life of Man.
The search has taught me that the search is vain.

103

How desperately some expect the dead
To answer their wild questions in their stead;
The empty space within the rotting skull
Prove more capacious than the living head!

111

Great Potter, on whose tool, a wheeling blue,
The world is fashioned and is broken too –
Why to the race of men is heaven so dire?
In what, Great Tool, have we offended you?

114

At the pale gate of birth an angel stands
Singing a lying song of lovely lands;
We listen for too long to what he says,
And life, real life, slips each day through our hands.

115

Would that some voice which knew the whole deceit
Far off in space the unborn soul might greet,
Hot-foot for earth, with lying fancies fired,
And blurt out all the terror and the cheat.

116

But what real thing could such a spirit be?
How far in space? What would there be to see?
We live in life; and not before or after;
And what scares some need not dispirit me.

117

Nor are those sightless stars a whit more wise –
Impotent silver dots upon the dies
The lords of heaven each night and morning throw,
In some peculiar hazard of the skies.

118

Let us make haste, perchance for us to warn
The eager soul that clamours to be born;
To rescue them from their tremendous doom,
Those fated generations still unborn.

119

Perchance to warn? And yet – for whom the warning?
What odd realm are these unborn souls adorning?
Fate's but a name for anything that happens.
Nothing can waken in an unborn morning.

120
Men talk of heaven – there is no heaven but here.
Men talk of hell – there is no hell but here.
Men talk of pasts. Men talk of what's to come.
Yet, all this talk is but two words: *Now. Here.*

147
Impassioned particles of dirt and sun,
Run your brief race, if one is being run.
Are we but shadows? Yet: I heard your laughter.
Don't say we had no purpose. I had one.

from *Second Best Moments in Chinese History* (1997)

Book One: *A Moral Victory for the Barbarians*

1
A slight rustle of leaves on a commonplace summer's day.
Two hours. Three hours. Four hours. Five hours.
A rustle of leaves on a nondescript summer's evening.
The poet suddenly rises and starts his journey home.

7
The scholars have gathered in a clearing in a wood.
Nervously at first, but with ever-growing enthusiasm,
They begin to discuss the insoluble problems of existence.
Soon, the forest resounds to their obscene drinking songs.

9   *Drinking Song*
'Hey, little girl: show me your genitalia!
Hey, young woman: show me your genitalia!
Hey, mature matron: show me your genitalia!
Hey, ancient hag: help me down from this tree, will you?'

20
A massively compassionate figure walks down from the mountain retreat.
At last the truth about the human predicament has been revealed to him.
Turning a corner, he trips over a fallen branch lying in the road.
He climbs nimbly to his feet, and continues swiftly down the mountain.

21

Sadly, the man crosses the bridge, followed by his daughter.
She tries to explain to him that it was all a misunderstanding.
He sighs, halts, and throws the monk's penis into the river far below.
Women, eh? Enlightenment, eh? Eh? Not to mention the water.

22

A muddy path in the north of the city
Eventually leads to an overhanging bridge
Which seems to link nowhere with nowhere. An occasional rustle
May be footsteps, but is more probably just trees.

25

Solemnly he wanders through the autumnal woods,
Outlining his views on immortality
To a silent companion, who, unknown to him,
Seduced his wife twenty-five minutes ago.

26

I trust these three clay actors, excavated together,
Do not exhaust the types available to them.
A judge and two men dressed up as women?
It suggests a certain monotony in the repertoire.

27

The Emperor and his seven lookalikes
Are walking down a palace passageway
On their way to meet the rebel messengers.
Every three or four steps, they exchange places.

30

Six sages are standing in a little garden.
Each has shut his eyes, and, by sheer absence of thought,
Has convinced himself that he has been absorbed into the universe.
An enraged servant-girl is about to kick one of them.

32

A sumptuous carpet lies in the garden
Behind the curiously eroded ornamental rock.
There is the imprint of a sleeping form upon it.
The sound of an argument drifts out from the house.

33

A few wet trees line the city lane.
They despatch their loads in occasional flurries.
Since moonlight is not shining on them, no-one is climbing them.
In an hour or so, moonlight will be shining on them.

45

A flurry of geese takes off from the low lake.
In an hour's time, their flight high overhead
Will enchant two people on a balcony
Which now lies bare, wet, empty, and wind-swept.

47

The silence of finished meals returns to the mountainside –
Except for the slapping of the scholars' ink-brushes.
Three men still writing about unreality.
But otherwise a quiet afternoon.

51

A few bamboo stems sway unimportantly in the wind.
There are three, or four – possibly five of them altogether.
No. To be quite accurate: there are six of them.
No, wait a moment – there are seven of them.

57

How little the shrimp thought at dawn, shrugged by the sea,
In its cold, legendary, saline indifference,
That fifteen pairs of hands would have touched it by the evening,
Before it was hurled with a yell of contempt over a garden wall.

76

Obviously the final day of autumn.
The last possible leaf is about to fall.
The last possible goose is about to enter the air.
The last boat is about to be left where it is.

83

Solemnly he wanders through the autumnal woods,
Outlining his views on immortality
To a silent companion who, unknown to him,
Is carrying a heavy metal bar in his sleeve.

89
The old man creeps towards the shaded doorway,
Furtively looking to left and right.
He goes in through the entrance and is lost to sight.
The sun continues its slow, silent game with shadows.

Book Two: *Darkness and the Occasional Traveller*

108
As he leaves the astrologer's house, delighted to have been told
That all the signs favour his immediate journey to the capital,
He trips over a garden rock, falls, and breaks both legs.
He crawls back into the house, to check one or two details.

111
The civilized man with the head of a large green ferret
Discovers that the door has been accidentally left unlocked.
Surely then, it should be possible for him to wander through the palace?
He looks carefully round the door, uncertain in his mind.

120   *Fragment*
When the Master was asked, how did he reconcile
His insistence on the need for a chaste, virtuous life
With his well-known penchant for having large servant-girls
Sit down on his face, he replied: Although *at first sight…*

141
Are the four thousand women in the palace today
The same as the four thousand who were here yesterday?
That would be an extraordinary coincidence,
Considering how many doors have been opening and shutting.

150

The phrase floats upward from the winding pathway
To the raised pavilion where he sits, drinking.
'I'll tell you what I miss most about impotence –'
Intrigued, he leans forward, but already they have gone.

159

A narrow path runs from the door of the small riverside house.
It runs through a fenceless garden and crosses a bridge.
It runs through a wood, then crosses another bridge.
It continues through the fields towards a bigger road.

161

The Goddess, taken by surprise in the dead man's kitchen
At his sudden resurrection, smiles disarmingly,
And prepares for him her first ever attempt at fish soup.
She has stopped smiling when she starts her second attempt.

171

A couple of Gods are staring at the horizon
In that way Gods have of staring when disconsolate.
The expression in their eyes might almost be human
Were it not for the fact that their faces are invisible.

173

The contorted pine-tree apparently changes its mind
Five or six times between the cluster of rocks
And the fullness of the air. Its topmost branches
Sway calmly in the wrong part of the sky.

187

Hearing of the defeat, the actor sinks to the ground, groaning.
Sobbing once or twice, he reaches into his superb gown,
Pulls out his penis, and indolently begins to tug at it.
A ripple of alarm stirs among the cognoscenti.

193

All day the unrelenting rain
Has fallen unrelentingly
Onto the garden where they should be sitting
Exchanging childhood reminiscences.

203

Why is he waiting in the audience hall of the temple,
Wearing such a strained, anxious expression?
After all, he is fairly certain that none of the Gods exist.
Hidden behind a screen, a tiny dog is checking a list.

215

The butterfly, newly awakened, refreshed by sleep,
Flutters into the bedroom of the philosopher.
Have I, it wonders, ever been here before?
Why do these slippers seem so curiously familiar?

217

The mistress and the maid have exchanged clothes.
They sit in the darkened room, sniggering quietly.
At length a heavy tread approaches the door –
The master! Or, certainly someone wearing his slippers.

223

By climbing out among the branches in his garden,
And inching his way with pained fingers along a high rough wall,
He is able to catch sight of her, seated on her balcony –
If she has bothered to come out and sit on her balcony.

246

The Goddess's face is slowly splitting open.
The other people in the tavern gaze over at her in horror.
A crack runs down her forehead, then on into her cheek.
Someone has badly misinformed her about laughter.

265

The hermit cries out suddenly in understanding.
At last he has remembered who he was
In the incarnation previous to this one.
He sets out for the village, swaying his hips.

280

It is exactly this house which he has dreamed of all his life.
Exactly that scatter of mountains in the distance.
Exactly that line of trees sweeping towards him.
Exactly that neighbour's wife coughing on the balcony.

300

A vast pleasure garden extends down one side of the river.
There is perpetual laughter in one room or another.
And perpetually the sound of someone closing a door,
And walking quietly away off down a corridor.

Book Four: *On The Eighth Floor of the Pagoda*

303

After sitting there for an hour or so,
The poet rises, gathers up his belongings,
Gives a last glance back, and leaves the pavilion.
As soon as he leaves, another poet enters.

329

Not only has the poet written a poem in this album –
He has also jotted down a brief evaluation
Of the character of the man whose house he was visiting.
The rare inscription ends with a curious abruptness.

330

A doleful song comes from the small house,
Abandoned among the mountains and the clouds;
Folded safely away in nocturnal forgetfulness.
Two voices? Three voices? Impossible to tell.

332

They have stayed awake throughout the entire night!
They have stayed awake, and nothing has happened to them!
Again the morning light startles the trees in the lane.
The neighbours various voices begin to be heard again.

337

An unrestrained youth is pissing in an alleyway,
Which leads to a road, which leads to a stairway,
Where a wineshop stands, in the upper rooms of which
An old man is wondering what exactly is happening to him.

342

He sits in the garden, appearing not to notice the rain.
How long does he mean to stay there? He must be drenched by now.
I am amazed that no-one comes out to talk to him.
Not even when it at last stops, an hour or so later.

357

Rain is falling steadily as they enter the village.
It falls steadily as they journey through it.
It continues to fall steadily as they leave.
And it still falls steadily long after they have gone.

359

The branches sway and, for an instant,
The woman at the window can be seen from the road.
But no-one happens to be on the road at the moment.
Or not quite at the right point on the road.

367

Breaking the silence which has reigned all morning,
A group of messengers bursts out of a doorway,
Disperses and disappears through the various exits
Of the courtyard which only the Emperor should use.

370

The four girls giggling in the remote palace room,
Trying on one ridiculous garment after another,
Are surprised when, after an hour, a cupboard quickly opens,
And a venerable ambassador hurries out past them, weeping.

371

Midnight in the outer rooms of the palace.
Cautiously a figure emerges from a box.
It strides over and inspects the various locks;
Then sighs, and returns quickly to its hiding-place.

386

Two ladies stand in a garden, smiling distantly.
How distantly? 7 provinces, 13 big rivers,
12,362 walls, and two buildings
In which great writers are at work. And now they've both gone out
    anyway.

387

Ah! That's a nice place! I would like to live there,
Thinks the monk, caught by a sudden view of a house
Nestling on the hillside. And, the next morning,
He does indeed wake up inside it, smiling contentedly.

389

The light streaming out from the small house,
From a modest lamp standing beside the window,
Manages to thread its way deep into the forest,
Thanks to the complicity of innumerable trees.

396

This bizarre artist paints by dipping his penis in ink.
The effects are more successful than you might anticipate.
Even so, his landscapes are probably finer than his portraits.
But his religious pictures are quite extraordinarily convincing.

398

The curiously realistic scroll picture of a desert
Begins to seep sand down onto the sleeping figure
Slumped over a desk beneath it, writing-brush in hand.
The level rises higher and higher beyond his ankles.

399

Rocks begin to fall out of the dreaming scholar's head.
A tree or two. A small stream.
Soon the room where he lies has become a charming landscape.
A party of drunks arrive, and sit down, laughing.

429

Having been kept waiting for almost a full hour,
The prince frowns as the Zen Master bounds out into the garden,
Wiggling his exposed penis, and shouting, 'I'm a bit of a lad!'
This had better presage a very great truth indeed.

437

The door closes behind them yet again,
And they retire once more into their private realm.
A subtle tactful breeze dislocates leaves on an elm.
The quiet passageway shivers now and then.

450

A full moon above the snowy peaks.
Dark, but everything is touched by brightness.
Late, but the universe seems about to start,
Once the last few finishing touches have quite been perfected.

460

Icicles rattle on the lower branches of the tree.
Perhaps an intruder has brushed against them.
Perhaps an intruder has not brushed against them.
Someone is noisily drinking his first tea of the morning.

461

What thought-provoking sounds issue from the sage's study.
Those mellifluous runs, elegantly drawn from a long-necked lute.
That gasp of surprise, and brief noise of tearing fabric.
That door slamming; that outburst of mature wise tears.

463

After reading through 90 canonical texts about purity,
The sage sighs with relief; stands up; puts
A melon under each armpit; looks round;
And hurries off to a place of greater privacy.

477

A pleasant afternoon on this empty road.
The occasional flurried shower, but nothing more
Disturbs the serenity. Then all is as before.
The tired genius on the verandah continues to snore.

482

Autumn. The old feeling of sadness
Assaults one as one turns the corner
Of the pathway above the town, to discover
That absolutely everyone seems to agree it is evening again.

484

Offhandedly scanning the latest census figures,
Which report 159,000 horses in the summer capital,
The palace official walks down a quiet corridor
To the empty office of his superior.

488

Now there is only a single point in the distance
To indicate the recently departed over-zealous tax-gatherer.
And now five other dots suddenly join him in the distance.
Well, so much for the recently departed tax-gatherer.

498

Somewhere in this house there must be an instrument
That will allow him to preserve this morning unchanged for ever.
Into room after room he goes, searching;
Out of room after room he comes, content.

501

Slowly dust floats down, onto the palace lakes.
Charred spars sink deeper into the lush turf.
Through the wide corridors runs an occasional surf.
Clearly, one of the final dynasty's final mistakes.

The Kuppneriad

1
And if there was a time before this 'beginning',
that would have been this actual universe too.
For what other totality can there be to belong to?

2
Another unwritten epic! They're my favourite kind.

3
as, from the end of it
poured out into the opacity of the night sky
an endless sequence of galaxies; of complexities
to be disentangled, at length, into galaxies;
into vast strands of matter, which could possibly
develop into life, or whiplashing enormities,
or currents which fifty lives, one after the other,
would be insufficient to cross. So it went on for

4
as I fell out the window of heaven, I remarked
the wonderful light of evening. Or was it morning?
Whatever it was, it was such a wonderful light.

5
Come out of that void at once. You aren't fooling anyone.

6

He rushed towards her, as if intending some indecency –
but whether she moved aside; or he unbalanced;
or both; or one contributed to the other;
or the gods finally lost patience with the gross self-
congratulation of those who call themselves monotheists –
he toppled over the side of the ornate balcony anyway
and landed in the midst of a still adoring throng.
And now, O Muse, let me begin my song.
There was at this time a certain young man
in the deme of Cowcaddens; and this good youth, hearing

7

His eyes flashed. He raised a powerful hand,
and pronounced the doomladen, ineluctable words –
until he had disappeared entirely beneath the bathwater.
Still she stood by the sink, calmly brushing her teeth.

8

His scream sounded out over the whole nonchalant earth.

9

Holding her close to me, I hacked my way
through the hostile ranks – but when I reached the door,
I discovered that she had vanished. Gritting my teeth,
I turned back, intently searching for clues –

10

How the Goddess sighed. Sometimes it depresses her
to hear what men most ask for. With a wan smile,
she disjoined another head from its cervical vertebrae,
and called out, 'Next!' I was pushed into the room.

11

I looked over, worried, to the source of the disturbance.
She followed my gaze and smiled. Don't worry, she said. It's nothing.
It's Dante. He keeps trying to break into heaven.
He seems to think he has some sort of right to be here.
Fortunately, we keep a troop of soldiers,
whose heads are little girls' bums, to watch out for him,
be alert for his arrival, and throw him out again.

It's a special detachment. No-one is quite sure
whether they have been rewarded for something, or punished for it.
On the whole, I tend to think they have been rewarded.

12

I sneaked back into the laboratory during the lunchbreak.
Yes! The experiment seemed to be proceeding
most successfully. In every dish of culture
a tiny God was growing. Oh! What triumph!
What an era this would be sure to inaugurate
in Mankind's spiritual pilgrimage towards the ultimate truth.
I assume I have time to nip out for a quick couple of sandwiches.

13

I was buying some food routinely in a shop –
when something in the tired but alert expression
of the girl behind the till jolted me into life.
Please do not understand this merely in a base, physical way.
She was bored in such an exhilarating manner!
To be anywhere else, at any other time!
Surely this was the Goddess? In disbelief,
I watched her carefully, for the least sign
that she recognized my presence and purpose. But no!
Some change passed from one being to another –
and nothing more would ever be shared –

14

I'm lucky. At least I still have death to look forward to.
But you! Well: what a predicament! What a predicament!
I'm not surprised you say you envy me.

15

It's just that I never like to see so much blood
coming out of a cake.

16

Know, then, this sobering gigantic truth,
vain, ignorant and autokulaktic man:
when God bends down in the bathroom, the very stars
weep at the acid, ineluctable sadness
somehow inherent in creation. And when he farts,
somewhere a little cosmos mysteriously disappears.

17

Knowledge of the numinous is a rare thing indeed,
and to be treasured, however it emerges.

18

Morning. The goddess comes quietly into the room.
She is looking slightly wiser than usual, as usual.
She is making no attempt to hide many of her subtleties.
Is a Divinity inviting me to apologise? Or the opposite?
I can lift newspapers up. I can examine new letters.
Look! Or don't look, if you are not here. Look there!

19

No; that is not true. You did not give me this body.
Rather, you helped create this body, and this
body unfolded as me. You cannot give things – who can? –
let me rephrase that as, even you cannot give things –
to what does not exist. Life is created,
not given. For what is already there, waiting
for life to be given it? Birth is something else.
Indeed – everything else is something else.
Sometimes merely another word. For nothing.

20

No you misunderstand me. I would estimate
that 40% of this crowd are not divine at all.

21

Of legs and women, oh Muses, sing; and of how,
as the light of the infinite morning crept in upon him,
the Deity slowly began to bestir himself
from the corner of the kitchen where he lay,
disbelieving among the disjected panoply,
on a soft, supportive mound of discarded (thoughts)

22

One o'clock again. Is there no prize this time either?

23

Our scene is the research establishment in Heaven,
where novel military inventions are constantly perfected.
A disconcerting giggling has just broken out
in the interior. The more astute passers-by
look at each other in ever-mounting consternation.

24

She broke my weapon off with a snort of contempt,
and continued implacably towards the inner sanctum
where our general waited for the information
that would let him work out what the Universe meant.
We knew we must, at all costs, keep them clear of there.

25

She dropped out of the sky, and landed in my bed.
I was shocked, of course. And grateful. But it was difficult
to keep up a normal, human conversation.
A certain strain intruded itself.

26

She opened her small mouth, and took out a globe.
It looked so stunningly like the earth, that I
glanced round involuntarily, checking that

27

She was sitting reading a letter when I jogged her arm.
The recoil smashed my inept skull, rebounded
from a wall, crashed through my pons; then ricocheted
from a mirror, whistling through my ear, and exiting
from my aghast nostrils, before burying itself
in the bowl of porridge in front of me. I sighed.
Obviously, this is not going to be my day –
cars or no modest cars beyond the sunlit wall.
Some mornings have it, and other mornings don't.

28

So, for hour after hour we traded impossible punches.

29

so I said to the four Goddesses, from my seat
in front of the small gas fire – Yes, I am most impressed.

30

So subtle, interlinked, and precarious
was the sequence of events which first brought us together,
that I often thought of how close we came to not meeting,
and felt a sort of horror at it. Now,
I still think very often of how close we came
to not meeting. But without the same horror.

31

So, the great heroes struggled for hour after hour –
wrestling, groaning, occasionally using swords –
loosing the occasional spear – and even, at moments,
firing off a few rounds of vocabulary –
while, in its little bed, the child continued to sleep;
oblivious of the mighty and epoch-making

32

Soon the bathroom was a hive of uproarious merriment,
with elbows and feet flying all over the place.
By Heaven, these old deities certainly know how to enjoy themselves!
You should have been there. You would have laughed to see it –
had you been sufficiently dead to be allowed entrance.

33

that friend, with whom he was locked in deathless combat,
the endless struggle between the good and the better?
Oh, wiliest of adversaries! At times like this
he even came close to forgetting which was which.

34

The Goddess's head instantly disappeared
into a round megaglobule of fat, from which
a neat little tongue continued to poke out, provokingly

35

The snake wriggled desperately, trying to escape.
But the woman caught it, tied it into a knot,
swung it round a few times, and flung it into
a rubbish-bin nearby. Having done which,
she picked up a piece of fruit, and turned on the television.
Soon she would have to make a *really* significant decision.

36

The veil that covers life is life itself,
she screamed, dragging me over to the window.
Remove the glittering surface, and what is left?
Some say, all that matters. But I say – Nothing.
By all means look for yourself. What do you see?
Oh, superficial infinity of fragments!

37

Then, after he had said this, he went back
to see if the ship was still safe in its harbour.
But he could not find it. Neither the ship nor the harbour.

38

Then, just perhaps as they start to believe
that no-one is ever going to come and fetch them
from the gradually more foully smelling clouds
that they are attached to: I'll turn them all to acid
and have them slowly, painfully eaten away
for an eternity. Does it sound impossible to you?

39

Though all discussion of this is root and branch inadequate.

40

Thus he was left alone, tied to the stake,
as night fell with more intensity than ever,
and his mighty organ reached out into the darkness,
questing, probing, ever searching

41

To be frank, I am almost bored by my own unearthly resilience.

42

We shrink, J, from approaching the ultimate in all things;
for fear that, gazing steadily at it from close to,
we shall suddenly think – so: this is all there is to it!
And at the final boundaries, what can we do
but turn and head back? We can hardly stay there.
Even he who may, with prospect of success

43

We sliced each other's head, brutal, from its neck,
then gazed at each other, astonished. Could this somehow
also lead to love? Might it still not be too late?

44

What exactly do you mean, 'The Empire has just fallen'?
Don't be so melodramatic. It doesn't suit you, Marcus.
Try to leaven all your remarks with a dry wit.

45

What joy! Look around, oh great ones! What joy!
The same appearance of a pack of worlds shuffled together!

46

Whatever it was, it was such a wonderful light.
I was almost sorry I was killing myself.
Or was it someone else killing me? I sometimes
have great difficulties with the details, I admit.
I heard a mocking voice call: 'Enjoy your fall!'
Or was that perhaps, not mockery, but the profoundest wisdom?
The difference is sometimes too subtle for me, I'm afraid.

47

Who could it be? Surely not a rescuer?
For who can rescue a God, from whatever predicament
he contrives, for reasons best known to himself,
to find himself in? He gave an Almighty groan,
so that the whole valley resounded in sympathy;
sniffed, and stifled some tears. How cruel life was!
Even to someone from whose body the entire

48

Yesterday I was still on the troubled elements;
as far removed from home, it seemed, as at any point
on all my previous tortured, absurd, long journeyings.

49

Yet nobody was sitting on the chair, again,
among the memorable suburban trees. Goodbye.

Note

When *The Kuppneriad* was first published, late in 1994, it was in a context in which one was requested to give a brief general statement concerning one's own work. Thus the note which follows was appended to it, which, though aware that in some ways it might be even more seriously misleading than I had hoped, I give here for the sake of completeness:

I am fortunate enough to be able to assuage any grief I have that my attitudes and interests should by and large be so remote from those of so many others, with the reflection that my past work does not particularly interest *me* either. It's a common enough phenomenon, I suspect. I further suspect that none of my past poetry offers a clear introduction to my work; nor does any of my present. Though I suppose I may be wrong. After all, the present offering contains some of the tragic remnants of huge past ideas which did not quite work. There will be more of them, no doubt. Since I wrote them, I suppose they might well be characteristic. As indeed might this.

Frank Kuppner